# BURIED
# treasures

BY COMMON CONSENT PRESS is a non-profit publisher dedicated to producing affordable, high-quality books that help define and shape the Latter-day Saint experience. BCC Press publishes books that address all aspects of Mormon life. Our mission includes finding manuscripts that will contribute to the lives of thoughtful Latter-day Saints, mentoring authors and nurturing projects to completion, and distributing important books to the Mormon audience at the lowest possible cost.

MICHAEL AUSTIN

# BURIED treasures

Reading the Book of Mormon Again
for the First Time

For information contact:
By Common Consent Press
4062 South Evelyn Drive
Salt Lake City, UT 84124-2250

bccpress.org

Book and cover design: D Christian Harrison
This layout makes extensive use of the typeface Cormorant,
by the talented Christian Thalmann, of Catharsis Fonts

ISBN: 978-1-948218-25-2
10 9 8 7 6 5 4 3 2 1

# Table of Contents

*Chapter titles are abbreviated.*

# Reading the Book of Mormon Again for the First Time

> I esteemed the Book, or the information contained in
> it, more than all the riches of the world. Yes; I verily
> believe that I would not at that time have exchanged
> the knowledge I then possessed, for a legal title to all the
> beautiful farms, houses, villages and property which passed
> in review before me, on my journey through one of the most
> flourishing settlements of western New York.
>
> Parley P. Pratt

IN 2016, I DECIDED TO READ THE BOOK OF MORMON for the first time in 30 years. The last time I read it was in 1986, during my mission to Central California. Our mission president challenged us to spend the week between Christmas and New Year's Day that year reading the Book of Mormon from cover to cover, which I did. And that was the last time.

At first, I didn't read it because I never got around to it. I had stuff to do. Important stuff. I was studying "Literature"—about which I thought very highly. And I had read the Book of Mormon several times before and during my mission. I know enough to get by, and even to teach Gospel Doctrine in three different wards. I read the lesson material and scanned the relevant chapters, usually during Sacrament Meeting, and I faked the rest.

And I read the Bible, almost compulsively, as both a Saint and a scholar. I wrote my doctoral dissertation on the way that certain 17th and 18th century British narratives re-framed biblical passages for political arguments. Much later, I wrote a series of articles, which became a book, about a strategy of biblical interpretation called "typology". And later still I wrote a book about the Book of Job. I found these biblical texts to be complex and rewarding, so I threw myself into their study, content that I was "studying the scriptures" the way one should.

At some point, I realized that I had been avoiding the Book of Mormon for years because I was afraid that it would not be complex and rewarding. I was afraid that it would not measure up—that I would find it simplistic and immature—and I was not sure that my adult faith could withstand that discovery.

For several years, this became a serious matter of debate between my various selves. After my mission I made it a point to study many of the world's great religious texts, but I had not yet, as an actual adult, read more than the odd verse or chapter of the religious text most closely associated with my own religious tradition. And the main reason for this was the paralyzing fear that I would find the experience unsatisfying and disappointing. And that kind of felt like fraud.

So, in 2016, I determined to spend the year reading the Book of Mormon and blogging about my experiences with the text. I wanted to take Moroni's promise seriously, both spiritually and intellectually. And I wanted to read the way that I had been trained to read—closely, intensely, looking for symbols and types and patterns. And I didn't want to throw any punches at all at the tar baby of historicity.

I know that a lot of people had done work on the literature, history, and doctrine of the Book of Mormon, but I didn't read any of it, as I didn't want to spend the year responding to other people's experiences with the text. I wanted it to be just me and the text, mano a mano—not scholarship, but rigorous, serious, close reading of a primary work. The very thing that I have spent most of my adult life doing and teaching other people how to do.

And because I wanted to experience the text with the fewest possible filters, I purchased an 1830 facsimile edition published by the Community of Christ—a version that reads like a book, with no verses, only a few chapters, and not even that many paragraphs. I wanted to wean myself from the scripture-mastery proof texts of my youth, and getting rid of verses seemed like the best way to do this.

I also wanted to try to experience the Book of Mormon the way that its first generation of readers experienced it— the ones who sold everything they had and walked across the country because they saw something in the book that mattered. Something motivated Martin Harris to put up his farm and his livelihood to secure its publication. Something struck Eliza R. Snow so forcefully that she donated her entire inheritance to help build the Kirtland Temple. Real people made real sacrifices because of this book, and I thought that if I read what they read I might see what they saw.

The forty-four short essays in this volume were all published on the By Common Consent blog between January and December of 2016. They are a record of my year-long engagement with the text of the Book of Mormon. I have made very few changes in the essays beyond some light copyediting and removing a handful of very dated references to political and cultural events of that year. These are not scholarly articles, or even well-thought-out personal essays; rather, they are the record of a deeply personal experiment upon the word.

The language of these essays reflects the immediacy of blogging—a medium in which publication is instant and feedback is quick and often brutal. They are humorous and occasionally irreverent, as befits a forum that draws readership through single paragraphs quoted on social media. And they are all fairly short, as any blog post must be, if it is to be read.

But they are also serious... and they show—I hope convincingly—that the Book of Mormon is a profound and complex text full of sophisticated narrative devices, recurring themes and patterns, and big ideas that can sustain a high level of critical analysis. Often, my conclusions map nicely onto the kinds of readings one presents in church talks and lessons. Sometimes, though, they do not. Sometimes, I find the prophets and narrators of the Book of Mormon to be disingenuous and wrong. Sometimes I find Mormon's redactions to be self-serving. And sometimes I read passages that are clearly presented as examples as cautionary tales instead.

But this, I believe, is what it means to take a text seriously as something written by—and about—human beings. In too many Church settings, the Book of Mormon is presented as a near-perfect record of near-perfect people saying and doing near-perfect things. That, in fact, is what I was most afraid that I would find—and that fear kept me away from my own spiritual heritage for 30 years.

To my great relief, I was wrong.

I discovered in the Book of Mormon a profoundly human record of people struggling with their relationship to God and to each other. It has all the messiness one would expect of a record compiled over a thousand years, with multiple narrative perspectives, biases, agendas, and blind spots—as the authors and narrators groped towards an understanding of the Kingdom of God. It is a book that can bear multiple readings from multiple perspectives without exhausting its treasures. And it is a book that Latter-day Saints should never be ashamed to place alongside the great books of the world's traditions—both religious and secular.

That, at least, is my story, and I will be sticking to it for the rest of my life.

Michael Austin
January, 2020

# 1

## A Book to Kill For

> There's a question at the beginning of this story: what kind
> of book is so important, what kind of story is so important,
> that you would kill for it. Literally kill. Well, this is that
> kind of book.

—Avi Steinberg, *The Lost Book of Mormon*

I HAVE LONG SUSPECTED that the main character in the Book
of Mormon is the Book of Mormon. It is a book whose primary
narrative arc tells the story of how it came to be a book—a
book about its own bookification. And though all books are
about themselves at some level (usually the level of the advanced
undergraduate English major writing a term paper), the level
of metafictional self-referentiality in the Book of Mormon is
something we normally associate with contemporary post-
Modern experimental fiction—or at least with *Tristram Shandy*
and *Don Quixote*.

The first chapter of the original Book of Mormon (which
comprises Chapters 1–5 in modern editions) serves as a

remarkably coherent introduction to the Book of Mormon's bookness. This would have been important to a reader in 1830. The first edition does not come with most of the introductory material that we are used to. There are no witness testimonies (these were placed at the end of the 1830 edition), no excerpts from the Joseph Smith History, no clearly worded introduction telling readers what they are getting into. The book does have a very short preface, though, explaining the theft of 116 pages of the original manuscript and the translator's instructions from the Lord not to retranslate the material. I quote it in its entirety here:

> As many false reports have been circulated respecting the following work, and also many unlawful measures taken by evil designing persons to destroy me, and also the work, I would inform you that I translated, by the gift and power of God, and caused to be written, one hundred and sixteen pages, the which I took from the Book of Lehi, which was an account abridged from the plates of Lehi, by the hand of Mormon; which said account, some person or persons have stolen and kept from me, notwithstanding my utmost exertions to recover it again—and being commanded of the Lord that I should not translate the same over again, for Satan had put it into their hearts to tempt the Lord their God, by altering the words, that they did read contrary from that which I translated and caused to be written; and if I should bring forth the same words again, or, in other words, if I should translate the same over again, they would publish that which they had stolen, and Satan would stir up the hearts of this generation, that they might not receive this work:

*but behold, the Lord said unto me, I will not suffer that Satan shall accomplish his evil design in this thing: therefore thou shalt translate from the plates of Nephi, until ye come to that which ye have translated, which ye have retained; and behold ye shall publish it as the record of Nephi; and thus I will confound those who have altered my words. I will not suffer that they shall destroy my work; yea, I will shew unto them that my wisdom is greater than the cunning of the Devil. Wherefore, to be obedient un to the commandments of God, I have, through his grace and mercy, accomplished that which he hath commanded me respecting this thing. I would also inform you that the plates of which hath been spoken, were found in the township of Manchester, Ontario county, New York. (iii–iv)*

This preface tells historians several important things. First, we know that Joseph Smith was so concerned about the prospect of the 116 pages resurfacing as part of a critical narrative that he chose to start out with a pre-emptive rebuttal. The preface also tells us that Joseph believed, probably correctly, that the impending publication of the Book of Mormon had been the cause of considerable speculation in the surrounding community. Its first generation of readers would not be approaching it as a blank slate, but as the subject of fanciful gossip and unbridled speculation. They would already have a set of expectations, most of which would not be fulfilled by the actual text.

It is also important to know what this preface tells readers—which is that they are about to be thrust, in *media res*, into a story that began 116 pages ago. Nephi tells us this right out of the gate:

*And after this manner was the language of my father in the
praising of his God; for his soul did rejoice, and his whole heart
was filled, because of the things which he had seen; yea, which
the Lord had shewn unto him. And now I, Nephi, do not make
a full account of the things which my father hath written,
for he hath written many things which he saw in visions
and in dreams; and he also hath written many things which
he prophesied and spake unto his children, of which I shall
not make a full account; but I shall make an account of my
proceedings in my days—Behold I make an abridgment of the
record of my father, upon plates which I have made with mine
own hands; wherefore, after that I have abridged the record
of my father, then will I make an account of mine own life. (1
Nephi 1:15–16)*

Nephi, in other words, wants us to know the same thing
that Joseph Smith wanted readers to know in the preface: that
the book we are reading has some gaps in it, especially towards
the beginning, where a part of the original story is missing. As
readers, we need to make some allowances for this as we engage
with the story.

Nephi tells us a lot more useful stuff about the book in the
first chapter. For one thing, he pegs it to a very specific time,
"the first year of the Reign of Zedekiah, king of Judah" (1 Nephi
1:4). Any reader familiar with the Bible will know that this places
the beginning of the Book of Mormon narrative just a few years
before the Babylonian captivity. Contemporary Latter-day Saints,
of course, learn this very early. But for the first generation of

readers it was a vital bit of information; this one fact demystifies the text by situating it in a known, or at least knowable, historical and theological context.

But the most important thing that the first chapter of the Book of Mormon tells us is that we are reading a really important book—maybe the most important book ever. To make this point, about half of the chapter (now chapters 4–5) is devoted to Nephi and his brothers' attempt to retrieve the brass plates of Laban—which would become the basis for the Book of Mormon.

The story is too familiar to need much of a gloss here. Suffice it to say that Laban, a Jewish priest, is the custodian of the plates that Nephi and his brothers—who are about to sail across the world to set up a new civilization in the Americas—need to get ahold of. If they don't, they will have no records, no history, no culture, and no scripture. More importantly (to us at least) we won't get the Book of Mormon, since the brass plates of Laban—the first records that the Lehites obtained and took with them to the Promised Land—formed the nucleus of the book we are holding in our hands.

Nephi and his brothers ask Laban nicely for the plates, which doesn't work (would you give up a priceless religious artifact to four teenagers who knocked on your door and asked for it?). They also try bribery, which Laban accepted without actually delivering the plates. And then, in one of the most famous scenes in the Book of Mormon, Nephi is constrained by the spirit of God to kill Laban, to impersonate him in his household, and to kidnap one of his servants at swordpoint to prevent discovery.

Nephi, in other words, acts in the most un-Nephi way possible in order to obtain the plates. In the first part of the chapter, Nephi is described as righteous, law-abiding, and devout. But soon thereafter, he commits at least three capital crimes (murder, impersonation, and kidnapping) to secure a written record that he has no legal right to—but that he must obtain in order for the civilization that he is about to create to survive. And, the narrative tells us, God approves—and even compels—these actions.

Thus, by the end of Chapter One, we know that the book we are holding in our hands is the descendant of a book that was so important that a blameless man was willing to kill for it, to kidnap for it, and to betray the core elements of his being for it. Readers in 1830, who had just paid the equivalent of $50.00 to buy the book from travelling preachers, found out in the first chapter that it was worth far more than they had paid. They understood the importance of a written record to the survival of a civilization. And they knew that they were in possession of a book worth killing for.

# 2

## Lehi's Vision as a Corrective Typology of Eden

HERE'S A THING ABOUT ENGLISH-PROFESSOR TYPES: we look
for symbols—and we are especially fond of symbols that go back
to the Bible. It's embedded in our DNA. When Tom Joad in *The
Grapes of Wrath* kills an overseer and flees into the wilderness,
we assume that he is destined to lead his people to the Promised
Land—because that's what Moses did. When a character gets
swallowed by a whale (I'm looking at YOU, Pinocchio), we assume
that he is going to turn his life around like Jonah did. It's just how
things always seem to work out.

The professorspeak word for this kind of symbolism is
"typology." A "type" is a story or other little snippet of narrative
that connects to an "antitype" in a subsequent narrative. Jonah's
three days in the belly of a whale, for example, is a "type"
that gestures to Christ's three days in the tomb, which is the
"antitype". Typology is one of the primary ways that the New
Testament connects itself to the Old Testament. Nearly every
major character or event in the Old Testament can be read—and,
for centuries has been read—as a type of Christ.

Like the New Testament, the Book of Mormon connects itself to the Old Testament through typology. Nephi, the younger son who is favored by his father to the dismay of his older brothers, is an antitype of the Joseph story in Genesis. The people of Lehi are saved from captivity by a prophet who leads them through the wilderness and to a Promised Land—an undeniable antitype of the Exodus narrative. Typology is as important to the opening chapters of the Book of Mormon as it is to the early chapters of the Book of Matthew—and that is saying a lot.

And then there is Lehi's vision of the tree of life, which takes up about half of the second chapter of the 1830 edition of the Book of Mormon (Chapter 8 in modern editions). The narrative arc of this vision—the act of eating a piece of fruit and being ashamed—is one of those stories that invariably focuses our attention back to a type: the story of Adam and Eve in the Book of Genesis. But there is a difference here—and it is one with profound implications for the way that we read the entire Book of Mormon: in Lehi's vision, eating the fruit is the right thing to do.

Let's look at a little snippet from each of the stories stripped down to its basic narrative elements:

| Genesis 3: 1-19 | 1 Nephi 8:18-28 |
| --- | --- |
| People are commended not to eat a specific fruit. | People are invited to eat a specific fruit |
| A force opposed to God tempts people to eat the fruit. | A force opposed to God tries to prevent people from eating the fruit. |

| Genesis 3: 1-19 | 1 Nephi 8:18-28 |
| --- | --- |
| Once they eat the fruit, they become ashamed. | Once they eat the fruit, they become ashamed. |
| The narrative validates their sense of shame and says that they should not have eaten the fruit. | The narrative rejects their sense of shame and says that they should not be ashamed for eating the fruit. |

I know that this leaves a lot of stuff out, but work with me here. The story in Genesis says that eating a particular fruit is bad, that people should be ashamed for doing so, and that fruit-eating brought a curse upon humankind. The story in the Book of Mormon says that eating a particular fruit is good, that those who try to make us feel ashamed of the fruit are not agents of God, and that the sense of shame, not the fruit itself, is the bad thing.

If we read this as a partial correction of the Eden story, it has profound theological implications for nearly two thousand years of Judeo-Christian thought. It suggests that maybe Adam and Eve were not wrong in eating the fruit—that they did something good and necessary, and that the resulting fall was necessary to bring about the existence of humanity.

The rest of the Book of Mormon leaves no doubt that this is exactly what Lehi's dream means. Later sermons will flesh out the idea that "Adam fell that men might be" (2 Nephi 2:25). This goes well beyond the traditional Christian notion of the "Fortunate Fall"—which means that God's goodness and power are so great that He can make even the catastrophe of the Fall work out to our benefit. The Book of Mormon suggests that the Fall of Adam was an unproblematically good and necessary thing—and that Adam would have sinned more by NOT eating the fruit than he did by eating it.

Using the connective logic of typology, Lehi's vision asks us to reconsider what we know about the Garden of Eden—and to wonder whether Adam and Eve might have been the heroes, not the villains or even the victims, of their story. Few Latter-day Saints realize the extent to which this would have been a thrilling, transgressive, and radically innovative way to read the Eden type in 1830. In many circles, it remains so today.

# 3

## The Book of Mormon and the Americanization of the Christian Mythos

WORLD-HISTORICAL MYTHS DON'T COME AND GO with each new generation. There are only a handful of genuine mythic narratives in the world, and almost all of them have been around for thousands of years. One of the things that great cultural narratives do is reconfigure the myths[1] of earlier cultures in such a way that their appropriation by more recent cultures seems logical and inevitable.

This has been going on for a very long time. Consider:

- The Aeneid (1st Century BCE): Written during the long reign of Augustus Caesar, Virgil's great epic tells the story of the founding of Rome by Aeneas, a prince of Troy and son of the Goddess Venus (Aphrodite). In the process of telling the story of Rome, Virgil incorporates most of the important elements of Greek mythology into the narrative of Rome's founding—assuring his readers that Roman religion was not simply an imitation of the Greek myths, but an important part of the same great mythic story.

- The New Testament (1st Century AD): The central point of the New Testament is that Jesus is the Messiah, or the "Christ", foretold in the Old Testament. The terms "Old Testament" and "New Testament", in fact, only make sense if one accepts this argument. Those who accept the New Testament, therefore, see themselves and their story as the logical and inevitable continuation of a much older culture's mythic and religious systems.

- The Quran (7th Century AD): One of the reasons that the Quran was able to unite the Arabian Peninsula under Islam in a single generation is that it constructs both Judaism and Christianity as earlier parts of a single great religious narrative of which it is itself the final chapter. The five great prophets of the Quran are Noah, Abraham, Moses, Jesus, and Mohammad—a clear narrative progression that culminates with an Arab prophet and an Arabic scripture.

- *Divine Comedy* (14th Century AD): The two main characters in the first two-thirds of Dante's *Commedia*, or The *Divine Comedy*, are Dante himself and the poet Virgil, who guides Dante through Hell and Purgatory. In much the same way that Virgil interpolated Homeric myths into a Roman context, Dante interpolated Virgil—and by extension all of classical antiquity—into the Christian story, uniting the two major myths of his culture into a single great epic poem.

- *Journey to the West* (16th Century AD): Written during the Ming Dynasty by Wu Cheng'en, the *Journey to the West*—

and its trickster/hero the Monkey King—has become one of the most famous narratives in the Eastern world. The core narrative tells the story of the 7th-century priest Xuanzang (who was an actual historical character), who journeyed to India to bring Buddhist scriptures back to China. *Journey to the West* is the story of how an Indian religion, Buddhism, became even more important to China (in the author's opinion) than the native religions of Taoism and Confucianism.

We see exactly the same narrative pattern in each of these stories: a young culture interpolates the myths of an older culture into a new narrative that shows how the new culture has been part of the story all along. This clears the way for the new culture to employ the myths without appearing (or feeling) like second-class mythizens simply imitating somebody else's religion.

This is all just a really complicated way of introducing Nephi's vision in Chapter 3 of the original Book of Mormon, encompassing chapters 10–14 in most current editions of the same. This vision, I believe, gets to the heart of what made the Book of Mormon so important to its first generation of readers. To put it briefly, the Book of Mormon does what all of these other great cultural narratives did: it takes ancient religious images and concepts associated with another culture and interpolates them into a story that makes the new culture (in this case America) the hero.

Nephi does this in several ways. First, the entire story of First Nephi is a typological reconstruction of the central narrative of the Old Testament: the passage of Israel from Egypt to Canaan. Like the Children of Israel, the Lehites leave a wicked city and wander in the wilderness for a while with God miraculously providing for their needs. Eventually they are lead to a "promised land," which, it turns out, is America.

Yeah, I know about Guatemala and Machu Picchu and the "two-Cumorah theory." But all that came later. Readers in 1830 were reading a book that (as they understood it) came from golden plates that had been found in America, by an American, describing an ancient world in which America was historically and theologically significant beyond their wildest dreams. This, of course, corresponded nicely to the sense that Jacksonian Americans had of their own specialness in the eyes of God.

As Nephi unfolds the future history of his descendants, their wars and conflicts, and the eventual discovery of the land by "gentiles," he is creating a narrative that brings all of the old religion into a context that readers in 1830 could recognize as their own. And as Nephi prophecies of things that are in the future to him (but in the past and present for American readers in 1830), he unfolds a sweeping history of Christianity in Europe dominated by "the Great and Abominable Church of the Devil"—a history that will ultimately be redeemed by Americans:

> Behold, after this, thou seest the foundation of a great and abominable church, which is the most abominable above all other churches; for behold, they have taken away from the Gospel of the Lamb. . . . And because of these things which are taken away out of the Gospel of the Lamb, an exceeding great

*many do stumble, yea, insomuch that Satan hath great power over them; nevertheless thou beholdest that the Gentiles which have gone forth out of captivity, and have been lifted up by the power of God above all other nations upon the face of the land, which is choice above all other lands, which is the land which the Lord God hath covenanted with thy father, that his seed should have, for the land of their inheritance; wherefore, thou seest that the Lord God will not suffer that the Gentiles will utterly destroy the mixture of thy seed, which is among thy brethren. (p. 30)*[2]

This sweeping vision, I would argue, is the beginning of a thread in the Book of Mormon that makes it similar to some of the greatest books in the world's history: the identification of the new nation of America as an integral part of the grand narrative that has dominated the Judeo-Christian imagination for thousands of years. The Book of Mormon did not create an American religion; it Americanized one of the world's oldest mythic systems. And to an American reader at the dawn of the Age of Jackson, this would have been a very big deal indeed.

## Endnotes

1.  I'm sure I don't have to say, because anyone who has gotten this far certainly understands, that the word "myth" in the context I am using it here means, "a comprehensive narrative that structures most of the smaller narratives within a culture". Calling a narrative a myth in this context takes no position on whether or not the narrative is true. George

Washington is a mythic figure. So is Superman—even though one of them certainly existed in history and one of them is entirely fictional.

2.   1 Nephi 26, 29–30

# 4

## The First Isaiah Chapters: The Book of Mormon as Biblical Commentary

THE DREADED "ISAIAH CHAPTERS" of First and Second Nephi
loom large in my childhood memories of the Book of Mormon.
My teachers told me to just skip over them and get to the good
stuff, and the general consensus of adults in the Church seemed
to be then (and still seems to be now) something like, "we all
know that this is the boring part of the Book of Mormon that
nobody understands, but great are the words of Isaiah and all, so
let's pretend that it means something significant and try to
sound really serious whenever we talk about it."

The thing is, though, that it really does mean something
significant—or at least something as bold, audacious and
spiritually thrilling as any act of biblical interpretation ever has
been.

With the introduction of these Isaiah chapters, the Book
of Mormon becomes a much different kind of book than we
have previously experienced. We have already seen that it is a
family narrative, a theological treatise, and a book of prophecy
with oracular dreams and sweeping visions of the future. And

it is a pretty good adventure story with a hero who kills a rogue and kidnaps his servant, breaks his bow hunting wild game, and builds a great seafaring vessel despite not actually knowing anything about boats. By the end of First Nephi, the Book of Mormon has also become a work of biblical commentary that presents difficult chapters in toto and follows them with a detailed critical analysis.

Even if he had been trying to confuse people for sport, Joseph Smith could not have selected a more difficult pair of Isaianic chapters to start with than Isaiah 48 and 49. Along with fitting uncomfortably with what scholars now refer to as Deutero-Isaiah (Isaiah 40–55), they also fit uncomfortably with each other. The first chapter, Chapter 48, is a harsh denunciation of Israel and a moral justification for the Babylonian captivity. In the course of rebuking Israel for its sins, Yahweh waxes poetic about what might have been if only the people of Israel hadn't been such faithless louts. This is Isaiah at his most Ezekielesque. He seems to be rejecting Israel in the name of the Lord and saying, in effect, "We're through. Don't call. I hope you like hanging gardens":

> [17] *Thus saith the Lord, thy Redeemer, the Holy One of Israel; I am the Lord thy God which teacheth thee to profit, which leadeth thee by the way that thou shouldest go.* [18] *O that thou hadst hearkened to my commandments! then had thy peace been as a river, and thy righteousness as the waves of the sea:* [19] *Thy seed also had been as the sand, and the offspring of thy bowels like the gravel thereof; his name should not have been cut off nor destroyed from before me.*

In the frame narrative, these words are being read to a group
of people who barely escaped the punishments it describes. The
tribe of Lehites in the first chapters of the Book of Mormon
is the remnant that will one day redeem Israel. This becomes
extremely important in the next chapter which is precisely about
the redemption of Israel by a saving remnant. This is where Isaiah
waxes poetic on the renewed and glorious land that Israel will one
day inhabit—a land that he called simply "Zion":

> ⁸ *Thus saith the Lord, In an acceptable time have I heard thee,*
> *and in a day of salvation have I helped thee: and I will preserve*
> *thee, and give thee for a covenant of the people, to establish*
> *the earth, to cause to inherit the desolate heritages;* ⁹ *That*
> *thou mayest say to the prisoners, Go forth; to them that are*
> *in darkness, Shew yourselves. They shall feed in the ways, and*
> *their pastures shall be in all high places.* ¹⁰ *They shall not hunger*
> *nor thirst; neither shall the heat nor sun smite them: for he that*
> *hath mercy on them shall lead them, even by the springs of*
> *water shall he guide them.* ¹¹ *And I will make all my mountains*
> *a way, and my highways shall be exalted.* ¹²*Behold, these shall*
> *come from far: and, lo, these from the north and from the west;*
> *and these from the land of Sinim.* ¹³ *Sing, O heavens; and be*
> *joyful, O earth; and break forth into singing, O mountains: for*
> *the Lord hath comforted his people, and will have mercy upon*
> *his afflicted.*

This passage has long been read as a Messianic prophecy and as
a bookend to the previous chapter. In Chapter 48, God rebukes

Israel; and in Chapter 49, he promises to one day re-establish the covenant and create a new Promised Land. The Book of Mormon's interpretation of the two passages advances the radical thesis that Isaiah did not (as pretty much everyone else thought) consider the Old World Jews to be the subjects of the prophecy. Rather, Zion was to be built in another place altogether and by a remnant that nobody knew about until the Book of Mormon came along:

> And it meaneth that the time cometh that after all the House of Israel have been scattered and confounded, that the Lord God will raise up a mighty nation among the Gentiles, yea, even upon the face of this land; and by them shall our seed be scattered. And after that our seed is scattered, the Lord God will proceed to do a marvelous work among the Gentiles, which shall be of great worth unto our seed; wherefore, it is likened unto their being nourished by the Gentiles, and being carried in their arms, and upon their shoulders. And it shall also be of worth unto the Gentiles; and not only unto the Gentiles, but unto all the House of Israel, unto the making known of the covenants of the Father of Heaven unto Abraham, saying, In thy seed shall all the kindreds of the earth be blessed. (1 Nephi 22:7–9)

Let us be very clear about the radical and shocking nature of this interpretation. It's huge. Earlier in First Nephi, the Book of Mormon associates America typologically with Israel and even suggests that the rise of the American continent was known to ancient prophets. In this passage, the Book of Mormon kicks it up to eleven and argues that one of the most potent symbols in the Old Testament—Isaiah's prophecies of Zion, the subject of countless poems and sermons and, like, half of the songs in The Messiah—refers exclusively to America and to the American prophet who would re-establish the covenant between God and an American remnant of the Israelite nation.

The impact on the first generation of readers, I believe, would have been immense: it would have shown them a story that they had known all of their lives without even realizing that they were its heroes.

# 5

## Lehi's Blessings: Type Scenes in the Book of Mormon

TYPOLOGY IS ONE OF THOSE BIG WORDS whose meaning changes with the needs of whoever is trying to make it mean something. It is a concept that predates the Christian Bible, but that has become extremely important to the creation of a single canon out of two diverse sets of narratives—what Christians today call the "Old Testament" and the "New Testament." Those of the Jewish faith, of course, see things differently.

A type is basically a literary allusion that works in reverse. Authors usually allude to things that have already been written. They can do this by direct reference, or they can take little pieces of an earlier narrative and construct a new story out of it—the way that, say, Pinocchio alludes to the story of Jonah by having its main character swallowed by a whale. Allusions can be extraordinarily complex, but they are pretty easy to understand once you get the hang of them.

Typology, on the other hand, moves from the earlier narrative to the later one—or, at least, interprets an earlier narrative as though it were a reference to a later one. If somebody were to find an early version of the Jonah story that claimed that the great prophet had actually been a puppet, for example, we might assume that the Old Testament had masterfully predicted the coming forth of Geppetto's only son.

To be taken seriously, this kind of typological connection—which Christians have long used to recast Hebrew stories as predictions of Christ—requires an author to know the future (which is not a problem when dealing with prophets such as Moses, Isaiah, and Ezekiel, since this was kind of the point). But type scenes can also occur within the same narrative—such as the betrothal scenes in Genesis 24 and Genesis 29, in which the hero (Isaac/Jacob) encounters his beloved (Rebekah/Rachel) in front of a well. These scenes connect parts of the same narrative together in ways that can be surprisingly profound without requiring anybody to have magic powers.

Which brings us to the Book of Mormon, which presents itself as the Third Testament of Jesus Christ—one whose narrative spans a history that corresponds to both the Old and the New Testaments. Both kinds of connective typology are present in great abundance in the Book of Mormon. The Book of Mormon connects itself to the Old and New Testaments through a number of clearly allusive narratives—several of which I have already explored. And a number of type scenes (such as the rise and fall of anti-Christ preachers or the migration of favored people to a Promised Land) repeat throughout the narrative in ways that recall the great type scenes of the Hebrew Bible.

The type scene that I would like to talk about now features both kinds of typology and much, much more. I believe that it is one of the most narratively complex passages in the Book of Mormon. I refer to the patriarch Lehi's final blessings of his children in the first three chapters of 2nd Nephi (Chapters 1–4 in modern editions).

The narrative in these chapters points backwards to Jacob's blessing of his children in Genesis 48–49. But they also point forward to Alma's blessings to his sons in Alma 36–42 and to the coming forth of the Book of Mormon in the 19th century. They therefore connect the Book of Mormon to the Old Testament, while, at the very same time, yoking Nephi's and Mormon's portions of the Book of Mormon to each other. And they do all of this in ways that reinforce the importance of the Latter-day Restoration in God's eternal scheme.

Let's break this all down.

At the end of Genesis, the Patriarch Jacob, who has been led into a new land by his righteous younger son Joseph, gathers all of his children together for a father's blessing. In this blessing, he settles the birthright on Joseph through his children Ephraim and Manasseh—the latter of whom was Lehi's tribal ancestor (Alma 10:3). In Chapter 49, Jacob gives a brief identity marker to all of his sons; when he comes to Joseph, he says, "Joseph is a fruitful bough, even a fruitful bough by a well; whose branches run over the wall" (Genesis 49:22). Latter-day Saints have long taken this verse to prophesy of Lehi and his family's journey across the sea and to the Promised Land.

Thus, this seemingly simple type scene connects the Book of Mormon to the Bible in at least three different ways:

It serves as a culmination of the story of Nephi as a type of the story of Joseph in Genesis—a story in which a righteous younger son saves his family by leading them to a place of security, while continually deferring to his father as the rightful spiritual leader of the new society.

It emphasizes the similarity of Jacob and Lehi's role as the progenitors of an entire people (Israel and the Nephites/Lamanites) who will produce an important book of scripture that testifies of Christ.

It highlights the fact that a portion of the original narrative (Joseph as a fruitful bough, etc.) can be read typologically as a predictor of the second narrative.

And we can deduce all off this without even reading what Lehi has to say to his sons.

Once we do read the words of Lehi's blessings, the typology becomes even more complicated—especially when we consider Lehi's blessings as a type of Alma's counsel to his sons later in the Book of Mormon. Lehi's blessings form a typological bridge between Joseph's brief characterizations of his sons and Alma's detailed counsel to Helman, Shiblon, and Corianton. Specifically, Lehi uses the blessings to make a number of important theological points:

In 2 Nephi: 1, Lehi speaks generally to his sons. He praises Nephi and tells Laman, Lemuel, Sam, and Zoram (and the sons of Ishmael) that "if ye will hearken unto the voice of Nephi, ye shall not perish." The clear favor shown the younger son reminds

us again that Nephi is an antitype of Joseph, whose brothers were
so incensed with Jacob's favoritism that they sold him as a slave.
Very soon in the narrative, Laman and Lemuel will try to do even
worse.

In 2 Nephi 2, Lehi blesses Jacob and, in the process, lays out
the doctrines of opposition in all things, the Fortunate Fall, the
Atonement, and free agency—all of which have become extremely
important elements of Latter-day Saint theology.

In 2 Nephi 3, Lehi blesses Joseph (who not coincidentally
shares a name with the guy who got sold into Egypt), and, in the
process, lays out the elaborate remnant theology that animates the
entire Book of Mormon. Basically, Lehi tells Joseph that his seed
"shall not utterly be destroyed" (66) and that another seer named
"Joseph" will arise in the latter days to bring a sacred book to this
remnant so that "thy seed shall not be destroyed, for they hearken
unto the words of the book" (68).

Once again, a whole lot of typological stuff is going on
here. Within the narrative of the Book of Mormon, Lehi is
foreshadowing the blessings of counsel that Alma will give his
sons, which call the errant Corianton to repentance, expound
and clarify key doctrines for the righteous son Helaman, and
encourage the righteous-but-lackluster Shiblon (clearly the Sam of
the Book of Alma) to keep calm and carry on.

At the same time, Lehi's blessings to his sons—especially to
Joseph—become prophecies of the Restoration. In fact, the text
of (what is now) 2 Nephi 3: 4–22 closely mirrors, and is at times
identical to Joseph's prophecy to his brothers in JST Genesis 50:
24–38—thus weaving the Biblical Joseph, the Book of Mormon

Joseph, and the Restoration Joseph into a single, intricate typological web of meaning and profound connection.

Let me just conclude by saying that I am not trying to use these passages to prove anything one way or another about the historicity of the Book of Mormon. I am not even slightly interested in that debate right now. Rather, I am trying to establish that the Book of Mormon employs sophisticated narrative strategies to connect itself seamlessly to multiple other narratives at the same time. True scripture does this. So does great literature. And it is a credit to the Latter-day Saints, I believe, that the "keystone of our religion" contains recognizable elements of both.

# 6

## Laman's Curse: Etiology and Race in the Book of Mormon

> For behold, they had hardened their hearts against him, that they had become like unto a flint; where fore, as they were white, and exceeding fair and delightsome, that they might not be enticing unto my people, therefore the Lord God did cause a skin of blackness to come upon them.
>
> And thus saith the Lord God, I will cause that they shall be loathsome unto thy people, save they shall repent of their iniquities.
>
> —2 Nephi 4 (1830 Edition)

ETIOLOGY IS THE STUDY of how things got to be the way they are. Religion and mythology are full of etiological tales. The story of the Tower of Babel (Genesis 11:1–9) is an etiological story to account for the development of languages. "How the Bear Lost Its Tail" is an etiological story about why bears don't have tails. We humans are naturally curious; we like to know where things come

from. And our emotional desire for explanations far exceeds our
rational capacity to discover true answers. In the absence of good
science, we are always willing to buy stories that just seem like
they ought to be true.

I say this as a preface to my discussion of an extremely
problematic passage in the Book of Mormon—the story of
Laman and Lemuel's curse in the fifth chapter of 2 Nephi. This
is a problematic passage for many reasons, but mainly because
it tends to produce really racist readings of the entire Book of
Mormon—readings rooted in a long and incorrect tradition of
seeing Laman's curse as an etiological tale to explain the origin of
Native American racial characteristics.

I want to make two points about etiology and race in this
passage that I hope will not be controversial, but that I suspect
will be because their combined effect requires us to acknowledge
both personal and institutional failures. The two statements go
like this:

When the Book of Mormon was first published in the 19th
century, it was seen by nearly everybody in and out of the Church
as an etiological tale—the story of how the American Indians
developed their specific racial characteristics.

Today, it is the official position of the Church that the Book
of Mormon is NOT an etiological story—or at least that it need
not be read as an etiological story—because the Book of Mormon
should no longer be seen as describing the only or even the
principal ancestors of Native peoples.

The first of these assertions is beyond serious doubt. Just
about everybody in the early Church from Joseph Smith on

down saw the Lamanites of the Book of Mormon as the principle
ancestors of the American Indians. Early Mormons considered
Native Americans to be the fulfillment of Book of Mormon
prophecy—a remnant of the House of Israel that was destined to
accept the Gospel and hasten the return of the Lord. And in the
process they were going to become white.

In 1830, there was hardly any other way to read this narrative.
In the first place, the notion of dark skin as a divine curse was
deeply embedded in the culture, both by a long history of racism
and by the biblical precedent of the Curse of Cain—which most
white Protestants in the 19th century accepted as the origin of
black skin. In this sense, we see biblical typology again playing a
key role in the reception of the Book of Mormon: for more than a
century, the Curse of Laman was read (incorrectly) as an antitype
of the Curse of Cain (which was also read incorrectly), and these
two etiological fables supported each other in the Church for far
too many generations.

This also had a lot to do with the state of scientific knowledge
in 19th century America. The first generation of Mormons lived
in a pre-Darwinian, pre-Mendelian universe that knew nothing of
genetics, DNA, natural selection, or even the ages of rocks. In this
world view, everything that people saw around them had to have
come about in 6,000 years in a universe that had no mechanism
for the gradual development of phenotypes. "God did it" was a
pretty standard etiology for all kinds of stuff, including racial
traits and socioeconomic conditions.

In 1830, there were very few plausible explanations for
racial divergence that did not involve divine intervention. The

imputation of etiological significance to Laman's curse, while in no way required by the text, was an unavoidable result of the cultural and scientific assumptions of the day. Today, however, we have access to much better explanations for variations in skin pigmentation. We no longer have to appeal to curse narratives that are morally reprehensible and scientifically unsound.

This bit about scientific soundness is important. God cannot speak to people in ways that go beyond their culture's understanding of the universe. Or, perhaps more accurately, when the scriptures speak to people about things that involve natural principles, we cannot understand what they are saying in terms that go beyond our culture's scientific understanding. When we have access to better narratives, we need to take advantage of them. And we usually do, though it can take us a while.

Let's look at an easy example of this phenomenon. In Joshua 10:13, we are told that the Lord, at Joshua's request, made the Sun stand still to give a military advantage to the people of Israel. We know, of course, that no such thing could have happened, since the Sun does not actually revolve around the Earth. If the Sun appeared still in the sky, the Lord would have to have made the EARTH stand still. But if the writer of Joshua had said that, nobody would have had the foggiest idea what he meant, since, for most of human history, thinking that the Earth moved around the Sun has been a sure sign of insanity.

Fortunately, a Church lead by living prophets has the ability to refine its understanding of ancient scriptures when cultural and scientific progress make new narratives available. This is exactly how the Church as an institution has responded to scientific evidence challenging the view that the Book of Mormon peoples were the principal ancestors of the American Indians. When presented with compelling evidence, the Church did exactly what we all must do when the things we think we know for sure no longer work for the world we live in.

In 2006, the official introduction to the Book of Mormon was changed from describing the Lamanites as "the principal ancestors of the American Indians" to listing them "among the ancestors of the American Indians." And the new Gospel Topics essay "The Book of Mormon and DNA Studies" makes it clear that the Book of Mormon need not, and should not be read as an attempted etiology of the Native American people:

> The Book of Mormon provides little direct information about cultural contact between the peoples it describes and others who may have lived nearby. Consequently, most early Latter-day Saints assumed that Near Easterners or West Asians like Jared, Lehi, Mulek, and their companions were the first or the largest or even the only groups to settle the Americas. Building upon this assumption, critics insist that the Book of Mormon does not allow for the presence of other large populations in the Americas and that, therefore, Near Eastern DNA should be easily identifiable among modern native groups.
>
> The Book of Mormon itself, however, does not claim that the peoples it describes were either the predominant or the exclusive inhabitants of the lands they occupied. In fact, cultural and demographic clues in its text hint at the presence of other groups. At the April 1929 general conference, President Anthony W.

*Ivins of the First Presidency cautioned: "We must be careful*
*in the conclusions that we reach. The Book of Mormon ... does*
*not tell us that there was no one here before them [the peoples*
*it describes]. It does not tell us that people did not come after."*

The "Race and the Priesthood" essay is even blunter about the
"Curse of Cain" etiological tale, grouping it with other discredited
racial theories and acknowledging that, "over time, Church
leaders and members advanced many theories to explain the
priesthood and temple restrictions. None of these explanations is
accepted today as the official doctrine of the Church.

This is a huge shift in something that once looked a lot like
immutable doctrine. Most Latter-day Saints of my generation—
who grew up with Tom Trails, the Polynesian Culture Center,
and the Lamanite Generation—have a hard time re-orienting
ourselves to this new understanding of race and etiology. We
never questioned the "Native-Americans-as-Lamanites" narrative
when we were younger, but we need to now. Not only has the
institutional Church cast serious doubt on that narrative. science
has given us much better ways to understand the evolution of
different skin coloring—ways that do not require us to be racist
jerks.

So it is up to us to find ethical readings for these stories
that have been read unethically for so long. When the "curse
narratives" of Laman and Cain are emptied of etiological
significance—when they are no longer attached to racist and
unscientific theories about skin color and moral worth—we are
simply left with stories about individuals whose moral degeneracy

took on physical dimensions. We can derive all of the meaning we need from the story by seeing it as an allegory of hypocrisy and the consequences of sin. It does not have to explain the concept of race in America to have spiritual meaning and value.

And we might profitably use this recent shift in what was once an important part of LDS theology as an invitation to show more humility about other things that seem unequivocally true today, but which may not seem quite so true tomorrow.

# 7

## We Talk of Christ, We Rejoice in Christ

Wherefore, as I said unto you, it must needs be expedient
that Christ, (for in the last night the Angel spake unto me
that this should be his name,) should come among the Jews,
among they which are the more wicked part of the world;
and they shall crucify him.

2 Nephi 10:3

AS A LITERARY CHARACTER, THE JESUS CHRIST of the Book
of Mormon operates something like Harry Lime, Orson Welles'
character in the brilliant 1949 noir film, *The Third Man*. Lime
does not appear until the film is two-thirds over, and he only has
fifteen minutes of screen time. But the entire film is thoroughly,
absolutely, unquestionably, and obsessively about him; nothing in
*The Third Man* makes sense without Harry Lime as a referent. So it
is with Jesus Christ in the Book of Mormon.[1]

The obsessive talking about Christ begins in 2 Nephi, Chapter
10. This is in Jacob's brief interlude in his brother's book, during
which he reads two Messianic chapters of Isaiah (50 and 51) and

discourses on the nature of the coming savior, referring to him first as "Messiah" and then, after a visit from an angel, as "Christ." Later in 2 Nephi, Nephi adds that the Messiah/Christ's given name would be Jesus.[2]

I have to admit that this used to bother me. A lot. It has always seemed so anachronistic to have Nephites and the occasional Lamanite talking about "Jesus Christ" hundreds of years before his birth—and expounding doctrines with an eerie relevance to 19th century religious debates. This is so different from the Old Testament, which never mentions the name "Jesus" (except as the character Joshua, who has roughly the same Hebrew name), and the idea of a Messiah has to be carefully culled out of references that may or may not have been originally intended to apply to the future. The Book of Mormon always seemed to me to be trying too hard.

But here's the thing that turned my thinking around: to read the Old Testament on its own terms [3] we must accept a lot more spooky stuff than we do when reading the Book of Mormon.

Let me explain: the traditional Christian interpretation of the Hebrew Bible holds that it speaks of Christ through the complicated discourse of typology. Its characters essentially live their lives as anticipatory symbols of New Testament events. To accept the Hebrew Bible as a text whose primary purpose is to testify of Christ (which is what "Old Testament" means), we must also accept that God manipulated several thousand years of human history in order to create some pretty vague narrative symbols: He told Abraham to sacrifice Isaac in order to point towards the crucifixion; He fed Jonah to the whale to prefigure the three days in the tomb; and He instituted an excruciatingly complicated system of animal sacrifice so modern Christians could read Leviticus and glimpse the truth about Christ's substitutionary atonement.

By contrast, to accept the Book of Mormon on its own terms, one must only believe that God told prophets about some stuff that was going to happen in the future—which, when it comes to prophets, is kind of the point. In other words: to accept the Book of Mormon on its own terms, we must only accept its own terms.

And Jacob's discourse about Christ in 2 Nephi is one of the most substantial discussions that we have in any of the Standard Works about what atonement means. And it is not just rehashing, either. As the following passage demonstrates, Joseph Smith was introducing some new and radical ideas about Christ's atonement:

> For as death hath passed upon all men, to fulfill the merciful plan of the Great Creator, there must needs be a power of resurrection, and the resurrection must needs come unto man by reason of the fall; and the fall came by reason of transgression; and because man became fallen, they were cut off from the presence of the Lord; wherefore it must needs be an infinite atonement; save it should be an infinite atonement, this corruption could not put on incorruption. Wherefore, the first judgment which came upon man, must needs have remained to an endless duration. And if so, this flesh must have laid down to rot and to crumble to its mother earth, to rise no more. (p. 79)

A religiously literate reader in 1830 would have seen at least three surprising assertions in this passage, which I list in ascending order of surprisingness:

That Christ's atonement was infinite in its scope and not limited to the elect, as most Calvinists believed. This was a major item of religious dispute at the time, and the Book of Mormon takes a definite stand.

That the Resurrection effected by Christ's atonement would be corporeal. This idea was not unknown at the time, but it was (and remains) unconventional. Joseph Smith, of course, would double down on this idea in a big way later in his career with the assertion that God himself is a resurrected and embodied being.

That Adam and Eve's Fall in the Garden of Eden was a good thing that had to happen for God to achieve His purposes—and that the Fall should be seen as a positive thing and not a negative one. Though there are precedents for this idea in the history of both Judaism and Christianity, it was not accepted by any denomination that I know of in 1830 and would have been seen as a radical departure by most practicing Christians.

In the historicity wars, of course, the detailed Christology of the Book of Mormon will remain a disputed phenomenon. One side will always see it as proof of a 19th century composition ("how else could supposedly ancient writers get Jesus's first AND last names right?"), while the other will continue to offer it up as an example of the inspiration received by Nephi, Jacob, and Joseph Smith ("see, this just shows what really good prophets they were").

But as I have said repeatedly, I am not interested in debating historicity. I am interested in the text that we have in front of us, wherever it came from, and in the fact the text talks of Christ, rejoices in Christ, preaches of Christ, and prophecies of Christ—just like it says it does. Whatever one's position on the larger issues of composition, it should mean something to say that the Atonement of Jesus Christ is the Book of Mormon's central theme.

## Endnotes

1. All analogies break down at some point. This one breaks down at the point of imagining Orson Welles as Jesus Christ. Some levels of disbelief are not suspendable.

2. Jacob's shift from "Messiah" to "Christ" is a less spectacular revelation than one might suppose, as they mean the same thing ("anointed one") in, respectively, Hebrew and Greek. Of course, "Messiah", "Christ", and "Jesus/Joshua" are actually English versions based on Hebrew and Greek words. And we have no reason to think that God actually taught Nephi and Jacob English, which means that the original words, under the book's own terms, could have been very different, with the translations owing to Joseph Smith's own linguistic and cultural assumptions.

3. By "on its own terms" here, I mean on the terms that it can be considered the Old Testament. The presentation of this group of texts as part of the Christian canon embeds the assertion that they, like those of the New Testament, are primarily concerned with teaching readers about Christ. When the exact same texts are considered "the Tanakh", or "the Hebrew Bible", they no longer convey this expectation.

# 8

## 2 Nephi and the Deutero-Isaiah Problem in the Book of Mormon

ONE THING THAT MAKES THE "ISAIAH CHAPTERS" of the Book of Mormon difficult is that the three major blocks of text are all read into the official record by different narrators at different times for different reasons.[1] They cannot, therefore, be adequately characterized as a single thing. The first group (discussed here), supports Nephi's argument (and Joseph Smith's too) that the Lehites are the saving remnant of ancient prophecy—Israelites who will survive the Babylonian captivity and re-establish Zion on the American continent. To argue that a prophecy is being fulfilled, one must cite the prophecy and explain its fulfillment, which is precisely what Nephi does in the first set of Isaiah chapters.

The second set has a very different rhetorical context. It is Jacob, not Nephi, who reads Isaiah 50–51 into the text. And he does so immediately after telling his people that he has seen a vision of the fall of Jerusalem. "For behold, the Lord hath shewn me that they which were at Jerusalem, from whence we came, have been slain and carried away captive," he affirms;

"nevertheless, the Lord hath shewn unto me that they should return again" (6:8).

Jacob's desire to mention the prospect of a return immediately after acknowledging the destruction gives us a sense of how difficult this news must have been for his people. They knew that Jerusalem was going to be destroyed—it's why they left town after all—but the fact of its destruction must still have affected the Nephites who left the same way that it affected the Jews who survived: it almost destroyed their sense of religious identity, their concept of God, and their understanding of themselves as a chosen people made holy by God's covenant with Abraham.

It is no accident, then, that the verses that Jacob reads from Isaiah were originally spoken to comfort the Jews who had been carried into captivity—and to assure them that their relationship with God was still intact:

> For thus saith the Lord: Where is the bill of your mother's divorcement? To whom have I put thee away, or to which of my creditors have I sold you? Yea, to whom have I sold you? Behold, for your iniquities have ye sold yourselves, and for your transgressions is your mother put away; wherefore, when I came, there was no man; when I called, yea, there was none to answer. (2 Nephi 7:1–2)

These questions are rhetorical, of course (and more than a little sarcastic, but that's Isaiah for you). The answer is that God has not divorced Israel, sold them, or put them away. They are the ones who broke up with Him. He remains their God, even though he has allowed Jerusalem to fall. And he invites the people of Israel back to the fold even as they are marching off to their captivity. God reminds them of their covenant and assures them that he has not forgotten:

> Look unto Abraham, your father; and unto Sarah, she that bare you: for I called him alone, and blessed him. For the Lord shall comfort Zion: he will comfort all her waste places; and he will make her wilderness like Eden, and her desert like the garden of the Lord. Joy and gladness shall be found therein, thanksgiving and the voice of melody. Hearken unto me, my people; and give ear unto me, O my nation: for a law shall proceed from me, and I will make my judgment to rest for a light thing of the people. My righteousness is near; my salvation is gone forth, and mine arm shall judge the people. The isles shall wait upon me, and on mine arm shall they trust. Lift up your eyes to the heavens, and look upon the earth beneath: for the heavens shall vanish away like smoke, and the earth shall wax old like a garment; and they that dwell therein, shall die in like manner. But my salvation shall be forever; and my righteousness shall not be abolished. (2 Nephi 8: 2–6)

Here, in one of the most optimistic passages in all of Isaiah, the prophet invites the Jews to re-establish the Abrahamic Covenant in their captivity—assuring them that, if they turn back to Him, he will remember them and pave the way for their return. This was an important message for the Jews after the destruction of Jerusalem, whether they were captive in Babylon or somewhere in Latin America building pyramids. It was the most important message in the world for the audience that Jacob was trying to reach.

When placed into the actual context of reception, these Isaiah chapters are neither daunting nor difficult: Jacob uses Isaiah to comfort the members of his family after he announces the destruction of Jerusalem. For them, as for the Jews who remained, Jerusalem was an ancestral homeland that conveyed a unique religious identity. Their religion was almost unthinkable without the Temple and the city that surrounded it. Jacob read these words for exactly the same reason that Isaiah first spoke them: to ensure a distraught people that God was still willing and able to redeem them.

But of course it's not quite so simple. These Isaiah chapters have long been seen by Mormonism's detractors as strong evidence for 19th century authorship, as they come from a writer (or, more likely, a group of writers) that scholars now identify as "Deutero-Isaiah,." or Second Isaiah (Chapters 40–55). Unlike the original Isaiah corpus (Chapters 1–39), which suggest an 8th century origin, the Deutero-Isaiah chapters all presume that the destruction of Jerusalem has already happened—and they speak directly to the survivors as survivors. It doesn't take long with a timeline to figure out that anything written after the destruction of Jerusalem could not have been on the Brass Plates of Laban, which Nephi and his brothers seized BEFORE the destruction of Jerusalem. This, in a nutshell, is the Deutero-Isaiah problem in the Book of Mormon.

To avoid grappling with this problem, many Latter-day Saints resist even exploring the view—now generally accepted by scholars in at least some form—that the Book of Isaiah has multiple authors and consists of texts written in both the 8th century, when the Assyrians were threatening the Kingdom of Israel, and in the 6th century, after the Babylonians destroyed Jerusalem. This is, they say, simply the result of secular scholars who don't believe that an 8th century prophet could have foreseen and reacted to events a century and a half in the future.

In his book, *Understanding the Book of Mormon*, Grant Hardy faces this issue head on, critiquing the positions of Latter-day Saints who dismiss the Deutero-Isaiah problem as "simply the work of academics who do not believe in prophecy." He asserts that this is "clearly an inadequate (and inaccurate) response to a significant body of detailed historical and literary analysis." [2] I could not agree more. But I also agree with what Hardy says next: that a more promising avenue for faithful Latter-day Saints "is to acknowledge that we probably know less about what constitutes an 'inspired translation' than we do about Ancient Israel. Once one accepts the possibility of divine intervention, the theology can accommodate the (always tentative) results of scholarship." [3]

The Deutero-Isaiah chapters in 1st and 2nd Nephi are an uncomfortable presence, but not an inexplicable one, for, as Hardy affirms, accepting a divine provenance for the Book of Mormon provides the theological basis to resolve difficult historical issues. And we do not have a very good sense of what it means for a prophet to translate sacred texts solely through inspiration—with no training in, or knowledge of, the original language.

And once we get past the discomfort of seeing something where we don't think it should be, we can appreciate the value of Isaiah's core message in these chapters—a message as comforting to us today as it was to the people of Jacob (and, indeed, the people of Israel): Even at the very moment when we are suffering the natural consequences of our worst decisions and actions, God loves us as a devoted parent and waits patiently, with open arms, to welcome us back into His Kingdom.

## Endnotes

1.   The three blocks of Isaiah chapters that I refer to are: 1) Isaiah 48–49 in 1 Nephi 20–21; Isaiah 50–52:1–2 in 2 Nephi 7–8; and the very long block of Isaiah 2–14 in 2 Nephi 12–24. A fourth block of a single chapter (Isaiah 29) appears in 2 Nephi 27.

2.   Hardy, Grant. *Understanding the Book of Mormon: A Reader's Guide*. Oxford University Press, 2010. p. 69.

3.   Ibid.

# 9

## Nephi's Desert Island Book: Isaiah 2-14 in a New World Context

> The mature Nephi is something of a tragic figure, cut
> off from his culture, despairing of his descendants, and
> alienated from his own society. . . . Imagine, for a moment,
> his situation. He was educated in Jerusalem and literate at
> a time when such training was rare. He seems to have been
> fascinated by books and records. And then in his teenage
> years he was suddenly taken from the culturally rich and
> intellectually stimulating environment of Judah's capital to
> live in a distant land, in the company of only his relatives,
> with a single text (the Brass Plates) to read for the rest of his
> life.
>
> —Grant Hardy, *Understanding the Book of Mormon*, 59–60

OUR UNIVERSITY LIBRARY SPONSORS a monthly "Desert Island
Book" lecture. The premise is pretty simple: choose the one book
you would want to take with you if you were stranded on a desert
island for the rest of your life. I gave the lecture about a year ago

and chose Oscar Wilde's *The Picture of Dorian Gray*. I thought a lot
about that lecture when I was reading the long stretch of Isaiah
in 2 Nephi 12–24, since the Brass Plates of Laban are basically
Nephi's Desert Island Book—the only reading material he has had
for more than 40 years.

Nephi's largest block of Isaiah, then, represents a distillation
of his years of study with the only book available. Afraid (and
with good reason) that none of his descendants would expend the
effort to understand everything on the Brass Plates, he excerpts
what he considers to be its most important section—a section that
treats the two most important concepts of his own prophecies: 1)
the possibility of Zion; and 2) the certainty of the Messiah.

### Zion & the Redemption of Israel

Isaiah (and we are clearly dealing with Proto-Isaiah here,
so there are no continuity issues this time) wrote during the
8th century BCE when Assyria was a serious threat to both
the Northern and the Southern kingdoms. Israel actually was
destroyed by Assyria in 722, and Sennacherib laid siege to,
and came very close to destroying Jerusalem in 701. So Isaiah's
prophecies of death and destruction were not exactly far-fetched
for his audience.

But Isaiah was unique among the death-and-destruction
crowd because he always combined his descriptions of Israel
destroyed with the vision of Israel redeemed. And he had a
special name for Jerusalem once it had been destroyed and then
redeemed. He called it "Zion."

The first section that Nephi quotes, Chapters 2–4 of Isaiah, constitute a single unit in the original text—one that perfectly demonstrates the way that Isaiah combines prophecies of destruction with prophecies of redemption. In this second set of chapters, he sandwiches a whole lot of strong criticism in between two beautiful and compelling visions of a redeemed Israel. He begins by describing how Zion will look in the last days:

> *And it shall come to pass in the last days, when the mountain of the Lord's house shall be established in the top of the mountains, and shall be exalted above the hills, and all nations shall flow unto it, and many people shall go and say, Come ye, and let us go up to the mountain of the Lord, to the house of the God of Jacob; and he will teach us of his ways, and we will walk in his paths: for out of Zion shall go forth the law, and the word of the Lord from Jerusalem. (2 Nephi 12:1–3)*

From here, Isaiah launches into a detailed description of all of the un-Zion-like things that the people of Jerusalem are up to. They worship idols, they allow people to go hungry in the shadow of great wealth, they refuse to bow down to the Lord—all of the standard stuff. And they will pay a great price for their disobedience. Most of 2 Nephi 12–13 is dedicated to explaining all of the ways that the people of Jerusalem will suffer when they are destroyed.

And then in Chapter 14 (Isaiah 4), he returns to the last days again and prophecies of the redemption that will come after the destruction:

*And it shall come to pass, them that are left in Zion, and
remaineth in Jerusalem, shall be called holy, every one that is
written among the living in Jerusalem: when the Lord shall have
washed away the filth of the daughters of Zion, and shall have
purged the blood of Jerusalem from the midst thereof by the
spirit of judgment, and by the spirit of burning. And the Lord
will create upon every dwelling-place of mount Zion, and upon
her assemblies, a cloud and smoke by day, and the shining of a
flaming fire by night: for upon all the glory of Zion shall be a
defence. And there shall be a tabernacle for a shadow in the day
time from the heat, and for a place of refuge, and a covert from
storm and from rain. (2 Nephi 14: 3–6)*

## Prophecies of the Messiah

Along with these compelling visions of Zion, the portion of
Isaiah quoted in 2 Nephi also contains the most fully developed
picture of the Messiah to be found anywhere in the Old
Testament, beginning with the prophecy that a virgin would
conceive a son who would be a sign from God:

*Hear ye now, O house of David; Is it a small thing for you to
weary men, but will ye weary my God also? Therefore the Lord
himself shall give you a sign: Behold, a virgin shall conceive, and
shall bear a son, and shall call his name Immanuel. Butter and
honey shall he eat, that he may know to refuse the evil, and to
choose the good. (2 Nephi 17: 13–15)*

The special role of this child echoes throughout the rest of the Isaiah section. In 2 Nephi 18, we see him as the king of Judah (note the pun at the end):

> The Lord spake also unto me again, saying, Forasmuch as this people refuseth the waters of Shiloah that go softly, and rejoice in Rezin and Remaliah's son; now therefore, behold, the Lord bringeth up upon them the waters of the river, strong and many, even the king of Assyria, and all his glory: and he shall come up over all his channels, and go over all his banks: and he shall pass through Judah; he shall overflow and go over, he shall reach even to the neck; and the stretching out of his wings shall fill the breadth of thy land, O Immanuel. Associate yourselves, O ye people, and ye shall be broken in pieces; and give ear all ye of far countries: gird yourselves, and ye shall be broken in pieces; gird yourselves, and ye shall be broken in pieces. Take counsel together and it shall come to naught; speak the word, and it shall not stand: for God is with us. (2 Nephi 18: 8–10)

And then there is this prophecy, still invoking the marvelous child. I dare anyone familiar with Handel's Messiah to read without singing along:

> For unto us a child is born, unto us a son is given: and the government shall be upon his shoulder: and his name shall be called Wonderful, Counselor, The mighty God, The everlasting Father, The Prince of Peace. Of the increase of government and peace there is no end, upon the throne of David, and upon his

*kingdom, to order it, and to establish it with judgment and with*
*justice from henceforth even forever. The zeal of the Lord of*
*hosts will perform this. (2 Nephi 19:6–7)*

You get the picture. Nephi pulls out nearly all of the potent
references to a coming Messiah—a child who will be born as a
sign from God, who will bring about the redemption of Israel.
Towards the end of the section, Isaiah ties his two great themes
together into the ringing declaration that it will be the Messiah
who redeems Israel and ushers in Zion: "Sing unto the Lord; for
he hath done excellent things: this is known in all the earth. Cry
out and shout, thou inhabitant of Zion; for great is the Holy One
of Israel in the midst of thee" (2 Nephi 22:5–6).

To understand why Nephi chose these chapters, out of all
the writings that we presume to have been on the Brass Plates,
we should keep in mind that Nephi knows that the very Jewish
art of pouring over ancient texts and isolating their meaning is
about to be lost among his people. He acknowledges that "the
Jews understand the things of the prophets" (2 Nephi 25:5), and he
admits—somewhat sadly, I think—that "I . . . have not taught my
children after the manner of the Jews" (2 Nephi 25:6).

As Grant Hardy explains, then, Nephi "sees himself as a
participant in a distinctive, Jewish mode of exegesis, though he is
the last one among his people" (*Understanding the Book of Mormon*,
61). He knows his people will only understand Isaiah if he gives
them the most crucial excerpts (as he does in 2 Nephi 12–24) and
then explains, in the clearest language possible, what Isaiah was

saying—adding his own prophetic vision into the mix (as he does in the remainder of 2 Nephi).

For latter-day readers, Nephi's excerpting of, and commentary on Isaiah does two important things: 1) it ties the Book of Mormon together with the Old Testament and shows how both, if read under inspiration, function as testimonies of Christ; and 2) it points us to the possibility of Zion—Isaiah's holy city that the Mortal Messiah would call "the Kingdom of God." Both of these things—bearing witness of Christ and working to build Zion on earth—were fundamental to the Restoration, and remain fundamental to Latter-day Saint spirituality today.

# 10

## God Is Good, and that Makes All the Difference: Some Parting Thoughts on the Isaiah Chapters in the Book of Mormon

IT HAS BEEN QUITE A RIDE through the three major sets of Isaiah chapters in the Book of Mormon, from the application of Isaiah's remnant theology (48–49), to the American continent in 1 Nephi 20–21, to the great prophet's words of comfort to the exiled Jews (50–51) in 2 Nephi 7–8, to the long block of chapters (2–14) in 2 Nephi 12–24, which tie together Isaiah's Messianic passages and his prophecies of a fallen Israel redeemed as the City of Zion.

These are difficult chapters—chapters that many of us have been taught to endure rather than understand. And as we begin to understand them, they just get harder, as both Nephi and Isaiah are doing a lot of complicated things at once. They are warning (and comforting) their people, predicting the future, testifying of Christ, and letting us know what to expect in the last days. And, for Latter-day Saints at least, they are doing all of this in 400-year-old King James English that obscures the fact that most of Isaiah is also poetry.

But for all of this, I believe, the dreaded Isaiah chapters all contribute to one great argument that we can state very succinctly, and almost everything important in our religion proceeds from it: that God is good.

Few people today will find this earth shattering, but it was really not a common belief in the ancient world. Nobody ever asked if Zeus, or Moloch, or Dagon were "good." What a silly question! Gods were supposed to be powerful. They were supposed to command respect. And they were supposed to take one's side in battle against other people and their gods. Moral goodness had nothing to do with the equation.

Under the accepted rules of Ancient Near Eastern theology, then, Israel's destruction by Babylon should have meant the end of their relationship with Yahweh. It either meant that He no longer cared about them, or, more likely, that he just wasn't up to a battle with the powerful Babylonian deities. Either way, the relationship should have come to an end right there and then.

But it didn't, and that changed everything. The figure we now refer to as Deutero-Isaiah said some remarkable things, which Jacob did us the favor of repeating in the Book of Mormon. He told the Jews on both continents that God was still God—that he still loved his people and wanted them to be happy. Isaiah extended a remarkable invitation to the Israelites: stick with God and renegotiate the covenant, and someday you will be redeemed. And the Israelites agreed.

The main theme of Isaiah is the redemption of Israel, and the name he uses for redeemed Israel is "Zion." This is why Nephi expends so much space on Isaiah's Zion chapters. But Nephi takes the idea even further. It is not just collective Israel that will be redeemed by the Messiah; individuals, too, will be redeemed by Christ. The redemption of a nation will become a symbol of the redemption of each individual. And the reason is the same: God is good.

As Latter-day Saints, we know that God is good, but sometimes we don't act like we know it. We often practice our religion as though the most important thing about God were His power and not His goodness. This makes God something to fear—somebody that we need to propitiate or else. . . . The principle requirement of such a deity is obedience, and the principle rationale for obedience is either the promise of reward or the threat of punishment. Humanity has always interacted this way with powerful gods that it fears.

What Isaiah and Nephi present to us is something so radically different that, even 2500 years later, most of us have a hard time internalizing it. They show us a God whose claim to our affections proceeds from His goodness instead of His power—a God with whom we can have a relationship based on mutual love, rather than a divine tyrant who will either give us stuff or make us suffer in direct proportion to how well we obey.

After 40 years of wandering, reading the scriptures, and communicating with the divine, Nephi finally understood the most important thing that Isaiah ever said: God is good. When modern readers really understand this too, we will never see anything quite the same way again.

# 11

## Nephi: The Anti-Isaiah

IF YOU JUST READ THE WORDS, you would think that Nephi was a huge fan of Isaiah. But if we look a little bit closer, we can see Nephi doing everything possible NOT to be like Isaiah in his own writing. Nephi "glories in plainness." Isaiah, not so much.

As soon as he finishes quoting Isaiah, Nephi starts to compare himself, quite favorably, to his prophetic predecessor. "Isaiah spoke many things which were hard for many of my people to understand," he writes, "for they know not concerning the manner of prophesying among the Jews." And rather than blaming his people for their ignorance, he acknowledges that he doesn't want them to understand how Jews prophesy. "I, Nephi, have not taught them many things concerning the manner of the Jews," he writes, "for their works were of darkness, and their doings were of abominations" (2 Nephi 25:1–2).

Let's pause for a minute to see just what Nephi is saying here. Immediately after quoting twelve full chapters of Isaiah, Nephi turns around and makes three remarkable points: 1) most of his people won't understand what Isaiah is saying because they don't understand how Jewish prophecy works; 2) they don't understand

Jewish prophecy because Nephi made a conscious decision not to teach them anything about it; and 3) he didn't teach them anything about Jewish prophecy because he thought that this manner of writing was implicated in "works of darkness" and "abominations."

It sounds like Nephi is saying something like, "Isaiah has some good stuff to say, but only if you read it right. Otherwise, all that obscure mumbo jumbo can be dangerous. And rather than teach you how to read it, I am going to say what Isaiah would have said if he were a straight-talking, plain-speaker like me"—only he says it like this:

> Wherefore hearken, O my people, which are of the House of
> Israel, and give ear unto my words: for because that the words
> of Isaiah are not plain unto you, nevertheless they are plain
> unto all they that are filled with the spirit of prophecy. But
> I give unto you a prophecy, according to the spirit which is
> in me; wherefore I shall prophesy according to the plainness
> which hath been with me from the time that I came out from
> Jerusalem with my father . . . for I came out from Jerusalem,
> and mine eyes hath beheld the things of the Jews, and I know
> that the Jews do understand the things of the Prophets, and
> there is none other people that understand the things which were
> spoken unto the Jews, like unto them, save it be that they are
> taught after the manner of the things of the Jews. But behold,
> I Nephi, have not taught my children after the manner of the
> Jews. (2 Nephi 25: 5–6)

And Nephi goes on to make the kinds of clear and specific prophecies that appear nowhere in the Old Testament. He announces the exact time that the Messiah will be born, what his name will be, and that he will in fact be the Son of God (2 Nephi 25: 19). As Nephi presents it, anybody who really reads Isaiah with the spirit of prophecy will be able to draw all of this out. But that would require knowing something about Jewish writing, which is too dangerous to teach his people. So he just tells it like it is (or, rather, like it is going to be).

And then Nephi gets plain and precious about a lot of other things too. In the closing chapters of his narrative, he gives specific rulings on several of the main religious issues of the 19th century American frontier, such as universal salvation (2 Nephi 28: 6–9), the closed scriptural canon (2 Nephi 29:1–8), the gathering of the Lost Tribes (2 Nephi 29: 12–14), and the necessity of baptism for salvation (2 Nephi 31: 1–12). It's like he knows just what we want to hear.

Since the very beginning of the Restoration movement, the specificity with which Nephi represents both the life of Christ and the religious context of 19th century America has been used as strong evidence of the Book of Mormon's 19th century origin. In his famous review of the Book of Mormon for example, Alexander Campbell remarks,

*This prophet Smith, through his stone spectacles, wrote on the plates of Nephi, in his book of Mormon, every error and almost every truth discussed in N. York for the last ten years. He decides all the great controversies—infant baptism, ordination, the trinity, regeneration, repentance, justification, the fall of man, the atonement, transubstantiation, fasting, penance, church government, religious experience, the call to the ministry, the general resurrection, eternal punishment, who may baptize, and even the question of freemasonry, republican government, and the rights of man. All these topics are repeatedly alluded to. How much more benevolent and intelligent this American Apostle, than were the holy twelve, and Paul to assist them!!! He prophesied of all these topics, and of the apostacy [sic.], and infallibly decided, by his authority, every question. How easy to prophecy of the past or of the present time!*

Before accepting this argument completely, though, we should at least consider that the foreknowledge that the Book of Mormon attributes to Nephi is no greater or more anachronistic than the foreknowledge that Campbell himself—and most other Christians of the past 2,000 years—attributed to Isaiah and other Old Testament prophets.

Those prophets, according to the standard Christian argument, had a sweeping understanding of the future. They knew that the Messiah would come in the form of a baby born in Jerusalem and that his ministry would be spiritual and not political. They knew that a Christian Church would be formed and would eventually cover the Earth. And they knew that Christ would die, be resurrected, and return again in the last days after a very specific set of events that they detailed. Anyone who really reads the Old Testament (so the argument goes) should be able to work all of this out.

The Christian tradition accepts unproblematically that Ancient Hebrew prophets had a full knowledge of the future and, for their own particular reasons, chose to communicate it in the form of vague types and confusing metaphors—and by choosing to live their lives as anticipatory symbols of the coming Messiah. Nephi believed this too, but he believed it with reservations. And he made a conscious choice not to hold his posterity responsible for Isaiah's words alone. He created a cheat sheet so that everybody could follow along.

I understand that this cannot be used to prove anything about the ancient origin of the Book of Mormon. Prophecies about things that have already happened are certainly not inconsistent with a 19th century provenance. But it is not a slam dunk. The Book of Mormon claims that an ancient prophet named Nephi explained clearly a lot of things that (according to most Christians) the prophets of the Old Testament explained unclearly. To see this as inherent proof of a modern origin, we would have to accept the argument that prophets are inherently bad writers—or that one whose "soul delighteth in plainness" has no business speaking for the Lord.

# 12

## Pride and Polygamy in Jacob's Temple Discourse

THE BOOK OF JACOB IS WEIRD. I say this lovingly, but it's true. It's not that the book says weird things. It's just that the things it does say don't seem to have anything to do with each other. It's more like a mix tape than a coherent narrative or a sustained argument about anything.

But the wonderful thing about Jacob as a narrator is that he knows he's weird. And he tells us exactly why his book does not have the kind of coherence that Nephi has trained us to expect. Writing on plates, he tells us, is really hard:

> Now behold, it came to pass, that I, Jacob, having ministered much unto my people, in word, and I cannot write but a little of my words, because of the difficulty of engraving our words upon plates,) and we know that the things which we write upon plates, must remain; but whatsoever things we write upon anything save it be upon plates, must perish and vanish away; but we can write a few words upon plates. (Jacob 4:1–2)

This is my favorite fourth-wall lapse in the entire Book of Mormon, and it creates a very different set of expectations for Jacob's writings than we had for Nephi's. Nephi comes off as a luxurious writer—somebody who has all the time in the world and can even afford to reproduce about one-third of the Book of Isaiah more or less verbatim.

Jacob, on the other hand, comes across as a busy person who wants to discharge his duty without devoting much time to narrative pleasantries. He does not resent his task, as some of the subsequent narrators appear to, but neither does he relish writing for its own sake. Nephi was a poet; Jacob is a pragmatist. This means that all of the information in the Book of Jacob comes to us through the author's "just the facts, ma'am" filter. It must be really important or he wouldn't have spent time chiseling it onto the plates.

This sense of critical importance should govern our reading of the temple sermon in Jacob 1:15–3:14. These words are presented to us as the most important sermon that Jacob ever delivered, and the legacy that he wants to leave with anyone who reads his book in the future. And his words are not pleasant. Right out of the box, he announces that God has commanded him to inflict pain on the Nephite people:

> *Wherefore, it burdeneth my soul, that I should be constrained because of the strict commandment which I have received from God, to admonish you, according to your crimes, to enlarge the wounds of those which are already wounded, instead of consoling and healing their wounds; and those which have not*

*been wounded, instead of feasting upon the pleasing word of*
*God, have daggers placed to pierce their souls, and wound their*
*delicate minds. (Jacob 2: 9)*

And what are the sins of the Nephites that have caused God
to command Jacob to pierce their souls with daggers? Seeking
after riches and marrying more than one wife at a time.

Seeking after wealth and tolerating deep inequalities was
pretty much the go-to criticism for Old Testament prophets.
When Jacob tells his people, "think of your brethren like unto
yourselves, and be familiar with all and free with your substance,
that they may be rich like unto you" (Jacob 2:17), he could just as
easily have been Isaiah or Jeremiah. Nothing is more common
in the Hebrew scriptures than a prophet of the Lord chastising
the Chosen People for seeking their own gain at the expense of
others. To a very great degree, exhorting people not to tolerate
profound inequalities in their midst is what "prophecy" means.

On the other hand, Jacob's long discourse on the evils of
polygamy at the end of Chapter 2 would have been something
completely new to the Nephite people. Monogamy in the Western
world was a Roman invention, not a Hebrew one. Before they
became part of the Roman Empire, the Jews—like most of the
other bronze-age cultures in the world—were a mildly polygynous
people.

I say "mildly polygynous" because, as in most polygamous
cultures, only elite men had multiple wives. Since males and
females tend to be distributed equally in human populations,
large-scale polygamy is an inherently unstable social system, as it

tends to produce an excess of violent, sexually frustrated young men. But there is no precedent in the Hebrew Bible for Jacob's assertion that "David and Solomon truly had many wives and concubines, which thing was abominable before me, saith the Lord" (Jacob 2:24).

Taken in its original Lehite context, the requirement for strict monogamy must be considered a stunningly progressive revelation—one that elevated the status of women miles ahead of the biblical standard by refusing to allow them to be considered simply sexual property.

So let's name the elephant in the room. Jacob's insistence that "there shall not any man among you have save it be one wife" (2:27) becomes cosmic irony in light of the fact that, just a few years after translating these words, Joseph Smith initiated the practice of polygamy—which the Mormons continued for more than 50 years. Indeed, anti-polygamist writers of the 19th century invariably quoted Jacob 2 as proof that Mormonism could not even live by its own supposed scripture.

But (as Mormons invariably pointed out in return), Jacob comes with an escape clause: "'For if I will,' saith the Lord of Hosts, 'raise up seed unto me, I will command my people; otherwise they shall hearken unto these things'" (Jacob 2:30). But this is not a get-out-of-jail-free card. Even if we give Jacob 2 the most pro-polygamy reading possible, the best we can say is that it commands strict monogamy as the normal commandment for a society and that, in exceptional circumstances, the Lord may command otherwise "to raise up seed."

While Mormons today tend to see something like this as a possible rationale for nineteenth-century polygamy, it was not presented as such at the time. The defenders of Mormon polygamy asserted it as a positive good and a superior moral and social system. They insisted that it was an inherent and unbreakable part of God's Eternal Plan. None of the leaders of the Church in the early Utah period—Brigham Young, Orson Pratt, John Taylor, etc.—saw polygamy as a temporary exception to a standing commandment for monogamy. Yet this is precisely how Jacob presents it in the Book of Mormon.

The only way to square the 19th-century practice of plural marriage with the Book of Mormon, then, is to agree that while the early Saints may have been acting under revelation from God, they did not understand the nature of that revelation. At the very best, they took a temporary expedient as an eternal principle and built an entire culture on the incorrect assumption that God's will for them could never change. If we accept it, this assumption allows us to reconcile the practice of polygamy with Jacob's strong endorsement of monogamy in his Temple Sermon.

This, of course, raises the inconvenient question of what other temporary expedients we might still be mistaking for eternal principles.

# 13

## The Allegory of the Olive Tree and the Conversion of the Jews: Jacob 5 as a Response to Romans 11

THE TEXT OF JACOB 5 INTRODUCES SEVERAL new elements into the Book of Mormon, among them: a new genre (extended allegory) and a new narrative voice (Zenos). It is difficult to see how this prophecy relates to Jacob's original audience, but it is easy to see how it relates to Latter-day readers, as it comments on, and partially revises, a passage from the Letters of Paul that has structured the relationship between Christians and Jews for more than a thousand years.

The passage I refer to comes from the 11th chapter of Romans, which I quote at some length here because it is really important:

> ¹³ For I speak to you Gentiles, inasmuch as I am the apostle
> of the Gentiles, I magnify mine office: ¹⁴ If by any means
> I may provoke to emulation them which are my flesh,
> and might save some of them. ¹⁵ For if the casting away of
> them be the reconciling of the world, what shall the receiving of
> them be, but life from the dead? ¹⁶ For if the firstfruit be holy,

*the lump is also holy: and if the root be holy, so are the branches.* ¹⁷ *And if some of the branches be broken off, and thou, being a wild olive tree, wert grafted in among them, and with them partakest of the root and fatness of the olive tree;*

¹⁸ *Boast not against the branches. But if thou boast, thou bearest not the root, but the root thee.* ¹⁹ *Thou wilt say then, The branches were broken off, that I might be grafted in.* ²⁰ *Well; because of unbelief they were broken off, and thou standest by faith. Be not highminded, but fear:* ²¹ *For if God spared not the natural branches, take heed lest he also spare not thee.* ²² *Behold therefore the goodness and severity of God: on them which fell, severity; but toward thee, goodness, if thou continue in his goodness: otherwise thou also shalt be cut off.* ²³ *And they also, if they abide not still in unbelief, shall be grafted in: for God is able to graft them in again.*

²⁴ *For if thou wert cut out of the olive tree which is wild by nature, and wert grafted contrary to nature into a good olive tree: how much more shall these, which be the natural branches, be grafted into their own olive tree?* ²⁵ *For I would not, brethren, that ye should be ignorant of this mystery, lest ye should be wise in your own conceits; that blindness in part is happened to Israel, until the fullness of the Gentiles be come in.* ²⁶ *And so all Israel shall be saved: as it is written, There shall come out of Sion the Deliverer, and shall turn away ungodliness from Jacob.*

Those familiar with Jacob 5 will recognize a lot of the elements in Paul's much briefer text. Both compare the House of Israel to a decaying olive tree that can be saved only by grafting in branches from other trees. Paul addresses the gentiles directly and tells them that they will, as Christians grafted into the Tree of Israel, become eligible for all of the blessings promised to the Chosen People. But they shouldn't get cocky about it because the Jews are still God's people, and their cutoffedness is only temporary. God's plan is for the favor granted the gentiles to spur the Jews to repentance so that "all Israel shall be saved."

Historically, these verses are at the heart of the Christian prophesy of "the Conversion of the Jews"—or the belief that, at some point in the future, most or all of the Jews in the world will convert en masse to Christianity. This belief was especially strong among English Calvinists, who believed that this conversion would have to occur before the Second Coming of Christ. It was on the strength of this prophecy that Oliver Cromwell permitted the Jews to return to England in 1656.

When the Puritans immigrated to the New World, they brought this belief with them, and it was a major part of the rhetorical environment in which the Book of Mormon was first read. "Nothing is more certainly foretold," thundered the famous American cleric Jonathan Edwards, "than this national conversion of the Jews in Romans 11." And this was largely the environment into which Joseph Smith was born, and in which he published the Book of Mormon.

If we read the Allegory of the Olive Tree carefully, though, we will see that it expands Paul's allegory in significant ways— namely, it adds the people of the Book of Mormon itself into the allegorical mix. The person presented as the original author of the allegory was the Prophet Zenos, a contemporary of Isaiah who lived before the Babylonian exile and who, therefore, saw "the House of Israel" as something more inclusive than "the Jews." And in the process of expanding on Paul's metaphor, the Book of Mormon reconfigures the classical Christian concept of "the Conversion of the Jews" and turns it into the more familiar and distinctive Latter-day Saint concept of "the Gathering of Israel."

Let us pause to recall that the Book of Mormon presents the Lehites as Israelites but not as Jews. Lehi and his family claim descent from Manasseh, not Judah, and this fact becomes crucial to our understanding of the difference between Jacob 5 and Romans 11. In its very basic form, the allegory of the Olive Tree presents four series of events that represent, allegorically, the four key time periods in the Book of Mormon's narrative of sacred history.

See Table: **Jacob 5, the Allegory of the Olive Tree**

Whatever one believes about the origins of the Book of Mormon, the Allegory of the Olive Tree in Jacob 5 is an extraordinarily complex work of literature. It is a narratologically complex text that introduces several embedded narrators (i.e. Mormon, Jacob, and Zenos) operating at different times and with different purposes to produce a single sustained allegory. It is a rhetorically complex argument that both supports and subverts an important biblical passage well-known to Joseph Smith's contemporaries. And it is a theologically complex passage that

Table: Jacob 5: The Allegory of the Olive Tree

| Allegorical Action | Time Frame | Interpretation |
|---|---|---|
| The Master has his servant prune the original tree heavily and then transplants branches to other places in the garden. (Jacob 5:8) | Before the Babylonian Captivity, at the time that Lehi and his family leave Jerusalem | This is an element of the story that does not occur in Romans, and it completely changes the nature of the allegory. Paul speaks of two kinds of branches, the original branches, which represent the Jews and the new branches, which represent the gentiles. Jacob's allegory uses both of these categories exactly as Paul does, but adds a third: the transplanted original branches, which represent transplanted Israelites who are not Jews (i.e., the Book of Mormon people). |
| The Master grafts wild branches into the decaying olive tree (5:10), and, for a while, they produce good fruit (5:18). | The New Testament / Christ and Paul | This portion of the allegory is very similar to Paul's parable in Romans 11. The decaying olive tree represents Israel, which, after the Babylonian captivity is represented primarily by the Jewish people. According to both Zenos and Paul, the gentiles, or non-Jewish Christians, are grafted onto the tree, becoming fully vested members of the House of Israel. |

Table: Jacob 5: The Allegory of the Olive Tree

| Allegorical Action | Time Frame | Interpretation |
|---|---|---|
| The Master notices that the original tree is once again bearing bad fruit (5:30–32), and, when he checks the transplanted branches, he finds that they too are bearing bad fruit (5:38–40). | The Restoration / Joseph Smith | Here we see a clear example of the apostasy narrative that has already been worked by Nephi. The original tree, which represents the various Christian Churches, has fallen away from God. This is a clear departure from Christian orthodoxy, though it is definitely presented as a possibility in the original Pauline text, which states, "Behold therefore the goodness and severity of God: on them which fell, severity; but toward thee, goodness, if thou continue in his goodness: otherwise thou also shalt be cut off". (11:22) But the descendants of Lehi—which the original text of the Book of Mormon clearly presents as the American Indians—are not doing much better, as they are also in apostasy and unbelief. |

Table: Jacob 5: The Allegory of the Olive Tree

| Allegorical Action | Time Frame | Interpretation |
|---|---|---|
| The Master decides to restore the original branches to the original tree by working in both directions: grafting branches from the transplant back into the original tree, and grafting branches from the original tree back into the transplants. (5: 60–67) | The Last Days | The conclusion of the allegory (well, except for the very end, when everything gets burned) invokes the "restoration of all things" and unfolds the wise plan of the Master from the very beginning. The original House of Israel has been divided for millennia, but it will be literally reunited—including both the Jews and the descendants of Lehi—as part of the Restoration of the last days. The allegory thus invokes the literal gathering of Israel found in the 10th Article of Faith. |

builds and extends the apostasy-and-restoration narrative that the Book of Mormon itself presents itself as a part of.

And it is yet another example for Latter-day Saints of the richness and beauty that our most distinguishing book of scripture yields when we approach it by study, and also by faith.

# 14

## Sneaking out in the Middle of the Night: The Anti-Exodus Type in the Book of Mormon

THE FIRST TIME THAT OUR FAMILY read the Book of Mormon, we used the four-volume children's version by Deta Petersen Neeley. After completing the second volume, I asked my ten-year-old son what he thought of it. "Well," he said, "I'm not sure what it means, but there sure are a lot of people sneaking out in the middle of the night."

As I thought about this, I realized that he was right. In the part of the book identified as the Plates of Nephi, three different groups of people are instructed by the Lord to sneak out of the place they are currently living and head into the wilderness. The whole Book of Mormon begins with Lehi receiving the instruction to leave Jerusalem (1 Nephi 2:1–4). Years later, as Laman and Lemuel are plotting to take his life, Nephi is told to do pretty much the same thing (2 Nephi 5:5–10). And finally, in the last book on the Small Plates, we are told that Mosiah was "warned of the Lord that he should flee out of the land of Nephi, and as many as would hearken unto the voice of the Lord should also depart with him, into the wilderness" (Omni 1:12). [1]

These three stories constitute a type scene, or a similar story told at different points in the narrative in ways that invite readers to compare them with each other. The "sneaking-out-in-the-middle-of-the-night" type scene ties together the various narrators featured on the Small Plates of Nephi. But it also joins the story of the Nephites typologically to the story of the Israelites in the Old Testament, who were also directed by God to flee from Egypt and journey to a Promised Land.

A number of articles on the Book of Mormon as literature have emphasized the importance of the Exodus type in the framing of the Book of Mormon narrative. [2] It is an important connection, but we need to be careful not to over-read the similarities. The differences are important too. In several key ways, the Book of Mormon revises and softens the archetypal story of a people directed by the Lord to escape from their enemies.

In the first place, the Children of Israel did not sneak out in the middle of the night. Their escape required spectacular intervention by God: miracles, plagues, the death of first sons, the parting of seas, and the drowning of armies. The Book of Mormon has very different optics. In all three of the Exodus type scenes, God whispers to a prophet that the people need to leave their homes and depart into the wilderness. And the people leave their homes and depart into the wilderness with a minimum amount of drama.

The more important difference, however, comes at the end of the journey. In the Bible, the promised land has to be emptied of its current inhabitants before the Israelites can inherit it. This leads to some of the most disturbing chapters in the Bible, in the books of Joshua and Judges, as the Israelites conquer the Land of Canaan and massacre its inhabitants.

In the Book of Mormon, the Promised Land is already empty. The people get there and set up a colony without committing a single act of genocide. They do not encounter anybody for some time, and when the Nephites finally do come upon an inhabited city (after sneaking out in the middle of the night), the inhabitants welcome them as cultural saviors and happily turn the government over to their king. Nobody has to die for anybody else's covenant with God.

When compared to the Bible, then, the Book of Mormon gives us a kinder, gentler Exodus with no fighting and no dying on either side of the divide. However, when we place these parts of the Book of Mormon into their nineteenth-century context, they become much more problematic—as they replicate the false, but common view at the time of America as an empty continent waiting for white people to colonize it.

Over and over, contemporary American texts describe the American continent as uninhabited, and nineteenth-century America treated it precisely as such. We "bought" a huge section from France, negotiated with England for another parcel, and "won" most of the rest of it from Mexico—all without concern for the population that had been there for centuries. This population was considered an inconvenience to be removed, and the removal was in many ways as brutal as the Conquest of Canaan. But in the collective imagination of the American people, the land was empty and the American Indians were the intruders. The white settlers were like unto the Nephites colonizing an empty land.

Not long after the coming forth of the Book of Mormon, the Latter-day Saints would become a big part of that colonization—beginning with their dramatic exodus from Nauvoo. Like most Americans, the Mormons conceived of the West as substantially empty. But they also believed that the Native peoples who were there were descendants of the Lehites in the Book of Mormon—and therefore a people to whom they had a moral and religious responsibility.

The Book of Mormon gave the Mormon settlers a perfect analog for their situation: like Mosiah and the Nephites coming upon the City of Zarahemla, the Mormons imagined themselves to be the cultural saviors of their Lamanite brethren—restoring their history and their sacred books, and expecting in return to be made their kings. Though it didn't always work out so well in practice, the Mormons did at least acknowledge the essential humanity of the Native Americans in a way that many American settlers did not.

This softening of the colonial imperative can perhaps be traced back to the patterns of population displacement in the Book of Mormon. The Exodus type in the Book of Mormon is a very real thing, but the typology is as much corrective as it is connective. The Hebrew narratives from the Exodus through the Conquest contain some of the most horrifying and indefensible passages in the Standard Works. And the bulk of the horror comes from God's decision to lead His people to safety in a land that is already inhabited.

In the Book of Mormon, the same God does pretty much the same thing over and over again without anybody having to massacre anybody else—which, all practical limitations aside, strikes me as a much better way to set the people free.

## Endnotes

1. More examples of this type scene occur in the Book of Mosiah—first, in Mosiah 18:34, when Alma and his small band of convert and are warned by the Lord that King Noah seeks their lives, and later, in Mosiah 22: 9–12, when the people of Limhi send a tribute of wine to the Lamanites guarding their city and, quite literally, sneak out in the middle of the night.

2. See, for example: George S. Tate, "The Typology of the Exodus Pattern in the Book of Mormon", in *Literature of Belief: Sacred Scripture and Religious Experience*, ed. Neal E. Lambert (Provo, UT: Religious Studies Center, Brigham Young University, 1981), 245–62; S. Kent Brown, "The Exodus Pattern in the Book of Mormon", in *From Jerusalem to Zarahemla: Literary and Historical Studies of the Book of Mormon* (Provo, UT: Religious Studies Center, Brigham Young University, 1998), 75–98.

# 15

## Was King Benjamin a Socialist?

> And also, ye yourselves will succor those that stand in need
> of your succor; ye will administer of your substance unto
> him that standeth in need; and ye will not suffer that the
> beggar putteth up his petition to you in vain, and turn him
> out to perish.

—Mosiah 4:16

MORMON LIBERALS LOVE TO QUOTE KING BENJAMIN. He
seems to validate the whole social-justice/safety-net program of
the contemporary left. He admonishes us to give to the poor, and,
like so many of the prophets of the Old Testament, condemns an
entire society for allowing deep inequalities in its midst. If there
are better liberal-Mormon proof texts in the Book of Mormon
than Mosiah 4, I don't know them.

Of course, this is no slam dunk. Politically conservative
Saints can always point out that Benjamin does not say that the
government should take care of the poor—and, in fact, he places
the responsibility squarely on the shoulders of wealthy individuals

to "administer of your substance unto him that standeth in need." If Benjamin wanted a social welfare program, he could have created one; he was, after all, the king.

This argument is like a chess game where both sides know the opening moves by heart and can go through them halfheartedly on the way to shouting a lot and tipping over the chess board. For centuries, Christians have played similar moves in their arguments about the ministry of Jesus Christ, who also had more than a few things to say about taking care of the poor, and who also did not ever directly say that this should be done by the state.

These have always seemed to me to be the wrong kinds of questions to ask. We know next to nothing about Benjamin's kingdom, including how (or whether) it had any structural way to take care of the poor. And even if we knew more, there is no possibility that we could meaningfully map our political situation onto that of an ancient tribal kingdom somewhere in the Western Hemisphere. Ancient scriptures were never designed to instruct us in the proper means of government.

They were, though designed to teach us (among other things) the proper ends of government. Ancient prophets regularly described, under the name "the Kingdom of God," what a good society should look like. If we are truly disciples of Christ, we should want to live in the kind of society that they described— which includes some structural way of caring for the poor and vulnerable. I have a hard time believing that anybody living in a democratic society could read the New Testament or the words of King Benjamin and come away believing that these texts completely divorce responsibility for the poor from the proper function of government.

But there's more. Not only does King Benjamin require us to become a society that takes care of the poor. He invites us to imagine a society that doesn't have any poor—one that is not inherently structured to favor those with great wealth, status, or political power. This is actually a difficult kind of society to imagine, since every form of government we have experienced so far always ends up structured to favor the rich and the powerful. It is much easier to work on alleviating the symptoms of poverty than to imagine a society without it. But this is exactly the kind of society that King Benjamin—like Jesus—asks us to believe in.

I do not mean to suggest that there is no room for disagreement about how to best accomplish the goals that Benjamin set forth. It is not self-evidently true to me that government redistribution programs are the best way to care for the poor, nor is it patently unthinkable that market-based solutions cannot do the job even better. Intelligent, moral, and non-crazy people can legitimately disagree about how best to accomplish the social vision that King Benjamin sets out in the fourth chapter of Mosiah.

But passages like these do take some political arguments off of the table. One argument in particular simply cannot survive a sincere belief in the Book of Mormon. Benjamin himself outlines this argument in Mosiah 4:17–19:

*<sup>17</sup> Perhaps thou shalt say: The man has brought upon himself his misery; therefore I will stay my hand, and will not give unto him of my food, nor impart unto him of my substance that he may not suffer, for his punishments are just—<sup>18</sup> But I say unto you, O man, whosoever doeth this the same hath great cause to repent; and except he repenteth of that which he hath done he perisheth forever, and hath no interest in the kingdom of God. <sup>19</sup> For behold, are we not all beggars? Do we not all depend upon the same Being, even God, for all the substance which we have, for both food and raiment, and for gold, and for silver, and for all the riches which we have of every kind?*

The claim that wealthy people deserve their wealth, while poor people are poor because of their own actions or innate characteristics, has no place in our religious or political discourse. Benjamin refutes it unequivocally, as did a long line of prophets from Isaiah to Jesus to Joseph Smith. We should view with great suspicion any policy or political movement that proceeds from such morally flawed assumptions.

One of the functions of prophets has always been to challenge us to imagine a different world than we have ever lived in. Isaiah, Jesus, and Joseph Smith all did this; they called that world both Zion and the Kingdom of God. King Benjamin does it too. Not only have these prophets invited us to imagine such a society; they have enjoined us to create it in a world where all of the models come from Babylon. This is not a task that we can defer to a millennial future. The responsibility to build Zion here and now inheres in the Restoration. The Kingdom of God is within us. And this is not irrelevant to the way that we participate in the political process.

# 16

## Those Wild, Ferocious, and Bloodthirsty Lamanites

LET'S RETURN MOMENTARILY to one of the most narratively complex passages in the Book of Mormon: the Record of Zeniff contained in Mosiah 9–22. I call this passage complex, not because its subject matter is challenging, but because it is processed through so many levels of narration. The record originates with Zeniff (who dies in the middle of it, implying a second narrator), and is then filtered through the story of Ammon (who travelled to the Land of Nephi to find the people of Zeniff), the redactions of Mormon, and the translation of Joseph Smith.

Narratives filtered through multiple perspectives are almost always unreliable to some extent. Great novelists use these filters to introduce different voices and possibilities into a text, allowing contradictory propositions to be equally true to the internal logic of a single story. Mikhail Bakhtin, one of the few really great literary critics of the 20th century, used the novels of Fyodor Dostoyevsky to demonstrate the tremendous rhetorical power of this approach, which he called "dialogism"—a bit of jargon that is almost (but not quite) useful enough to justify the pretension of its existence.

I want to keep this narrative unreliability in mind as we look at one of the first things that Zeniff tells us in his narrative: that the Lamanites have become a wild and blood-thirsty people:

> *Now, the Lamanites knew nothing concerning the Lord, nor the strength of the Lord, therefore they depended upon their own strength. Yet they were a strong people, as to the strength of men. They were a wild, and ferocious, and a blood-thirsty people, believing in the tradition of their fathers. (Mosiah 10: 11–12)*

The Nephites, in other words, are good, civilized, religious, and enlightened—while the Lamanites are uncivilized savages who drink human blood from the skulls of their vanquished enemies. Americans in the Age of Andrew Jackson knew this story well; they used it to justify genocide. And this characterization is extremely important to the Book of Mormon narrative, as it is the first thing that readers learn about the Lamanites after they have been off the stage for nearly 400 years. It is a damning first impression.

But it is not an accurate one—not even by the terms of the narrative in which it appears. This is not to say that these are not bloody chapters of the Book of Mormon. They are. But nearly all of the bloodthirsting in them comes from the Nephites, not the Lamanites. Here are just three examples of some of the most "wild, ferocious, and bloodthirsty" stuff that we see in the entire

Book of Mormon—and the Nephites did it all. The first two come from the Record of Zeniff, and the last one comes from later on in the Book of Alma:

Zeniff's son, Noah, sets up a corrupt court and becomes a tyrant. When the prophet Abininadi comes (as prophets invariably do) to call the king and court to repentance, they have a theological dispute with him and then burn him alive (Mosiah 17).

Later in the same story, when the Priests of Noah are forced to flee the city, they kidnap and rape the daughters of the Lamanites (Mosiah 20).

Much later, in the Book of Alma, Alma and Amulek preach the gospel to people in the Nephite city of Ammonihah. Many of the women and children of Ammonihah believe and are baptized, for which the other Ammonihahans gather them together and burn them alive (Alma 14).

Abduction, rape, and burning alive are pretty much what people mean when they say "wild and bloodthirsty," yet it is invariably the civilized Nephites, rather than the supposedly bloodthirsty Lamanites, who engage in these activities. When Ammon goes into the land of the Lamanites to preach the gospel (a story that is the narrative parallel to Alma in Ammonihah), he is treated as an honored guest and offered the king's daughter's hand in marriage.

The story of the civilized Nephites and the bloodthirsty Lamanites does not survive close reading of the text, yet it remains one of the things that most people take away from their first reading of the Book of Mormon—largely because of descriptions like the one in the Record of Zeniff. This is why it is so important to look at things like narrative perspective and unreliability in the text. But this way of reading a scripture often makes us uncomfortable by working against our normal study technique of treating every verse of the Book of Mormon like the unfiltered word of God and proof-texting accordingly.

But this is not how the Book of Mormon presents itself to its readers. By its own account, the Book of Mormon is a complex history of a thousand-year civilization. If we want to believe that it is anything like what it claims to be, we have to acknowledge that its narrators have the same limits that all human beings have and that its narrative complexity does not (because it cannot) give us unfiltered historical or theological truth. That's just not how multi-perspectival narratives work. If we want to believe that the Book of Mormon is a real historical record, we have to acknowledge that it has the same kinds of biases and blind spots that historical records always have. This is what it means to be "historical."

In the example above, the narrator closest to the events (Zeniff) has an extremely limited perspective on Nephite-Lamanite relations, and the principal redactor (Mormon) has spent his life fighting a hopeless war against the Lamanites of his own day. Furthermore, the translator, Joseph Smith, lived in a country that was actively depriving the natives—whom he equated with the Lamanites—of their lands and livelihoods. These are exactly the kinds of perspectives that can introduce bias into a narrative. And really reading the scriptures means understanding how this kind of stuff works.

# 17

## Alma, the Dunbar Number, and the Waters of Mormon First Ward

> And after this manner he did baptize every one that went
> forth to the place of Mormon; and they were in number
> about two hundred and four souls; yea, and they were
> baptized in the waters of Mormon, and were filled with the
> grace of God.

—Mosiah 18:16

OVER THE LAST EIGHT YEARS my family has belonged to three
different wards. We didn't move. The ward boundaries moved
around us, but we had very different experiences in each ward,
which I am convinced had something to do with the size of each
congregation. The narrative arc follows, albeit not sequentially,
the story of Goldilocks and the Three Bears: one ward was too big,
one was too small, and one was just right.

The "too big" ward had an average Sacrament Meeting
attendance of more than 250 people. We always opened up the
curtains and went halfway to the back of the cultural hall. We

spent nearly two years in that ward without really getting to know anybody very well. Neither my wife nor I had a calling, we rarely did anything with people outside of church, and I am pretty sure that the bishop didn't know my name. In the "too small" ward—with an average sacrament attendance under 100—everybody was too busy to have relationships with each other. Most people had multiple callings. People burned out quickly. And the Same Ten People ended up doing everything.

And then there was the "just right" ward, with an average Sacrament Meeting attendance of between 150 and 175 people—one of the most nurturing and supportive wards I have ever been part of. People became good friends with each other. We became involved in each other's lives to an extent that I have never before experienced. We raised each other's children, had Family Home Evenings together, and I even went to my first and only "Super Bowl Party" after church one day. I watched all seven innings. It was that good.

How much did these experiences have to do with the number of people in the ward? There is no way to tell for sure, but a lot of fascinating research has been done on the ideal size of human communities. In the 1990s, the British anthropologist and primatologist Robin Dunbar proposed that human beings can maintain stable relationships with about 150 other people in non-coercive communities. He estimated that this was the ideal size of the hunter-gatherer communities in which we evolved. Subsequent research has pushed the "Dunbar Number" as high as 250, with most scholars settling somewhere between 150–200.

The Dunbar Number works on the principle that every extra person in a community doubles the cognitive resources necessary to be a part of it—since being part of a community means keeping track of all of the different ways that every member of that community interacts with every other member. The cognitive power to keep track of 150 or 200 other people in this way is staggering. Some believe that this is the main reason that humans evolved such big brains in the first place. And communities that exceed this number necessarily become coercive, top-down, and rule-governed—there is simply no other way to keep track of everybody.

So all of this was going through my mind when I noticed that Mosiah 18—which is the pivotal chapter about the founding of the Nephite church—not only names names; it numbers numbers: "they were in number about two hundred and four souls." First off, who says, "about 204"? People say "about 200," but 204 is more like an exact count. And it is an exact count that is exactly in line with what modern scientists believe about the ideal size of a human community.

And it is roughly the size of most of the LDS wards that I have belonged to. I can't help but think that this says something about what a ward is supposed to be. We are not simply called to worship alongside one another. In the very same chapter of Mosiah, we are called to mourn with those that mourn, comfort those that stand in need of comfort, and bear one another's burdens that they may be light. We are called, in other words, to be part of each other. There are rigid cognitive limits on how many people we can know that well.

Loving everybody in the world is easy because it is an abstract love. We can't be part of everybody in the way that the Gospel calls us to be. We don't know how. Our wards are the places that we learn how to do this with a manageable number of people—most of whom (if the system is working) aren't very much like us. This is not quite Zion. But it is a training ground for Zion, which we can only build when we have learned the lessons that are available in the local communities that we have covenanted to build.

# 18

## Alma at the Waters of Mormon: What it Meant to Belong to the World's First Church

AS THE CHRONICLE OF A FAILED COLONY, the Record of Zeniff takes up way too much space in the Book of Mormon. Readers of Mosiah must be forgiven, therefore, if they fail to recognize the magnitude of what happens in Chapter 18. To put it simply, Alma's founding of a Church at the Waters of Mormon is the most significant thing that happens in the entire Book of Mormon, with the single exception of the appearance of Jesus Christ in 3 Nephi. If we accept this passage as historical, then we must see Alma's actions in Mosiah 18 as creating the world's first "church" in any modern sense of the word.

There is no ancient precedent for what we call a "church." The Ancient Israelites did not have a church. They had an official state deity and a set of cultic practices centering around the temple.

(The Greeks had pretty much the same thing but with more wine and better plays). To the extent that "religion" existed anywhere in the ancient world, it was a collective affair: Israel pleased, or failed to please Yahweh, but no individual Israelite ever got to decide which church to belong to. Before Alma's creation of the Church at the Waters of Mormon, this was how it seemed to work among the Nephites.

About 200 years after the events described in Mosiah, the Apostle Paul went through the holy land setting up Christian Churches in the major cities of Asia Minor. Lacking a word for such an assembly, the New Testament writers used the Greek word *ekklesia*, which simply meant "assembly," to describe what Paul and others set up. From this word, of course, we get "ecclesiastical" with all of its derivatives—and translated into English it became "church," a concept that originated (it has generally been assumed) with the first generation of urban Christians.

But if we accept the historical claims of the Book of Mormon, we need to push the origins of the *ekklesia* back to the time of Alma. And this actually gives us some very useful information for understanding the concept. Mosiah 18 is especially useful in defining the boundaries of roughly the same kind of ecclesiastical community created by Paul. Through the baptismal covenant in 18:8–10, Alma sets out a sort of *Mere Christianity* much mere-er than C.S. Lewis ever imagined:

> And it came to pass that he said unto them: Behold, here are
> the waters of Mormon (for thus were they called) and now, as
> ye are desirous to come into the fold of God, and to be called
> his people, and are willing to bear one another's burdens, that
> they may be light; Yea, and are willing to mourn with those that
> mourn; yea, and comfort those that stand in need of comfort,
> and to stand as witnesses of God at all times and in all things,

*and in all places that ye may be in, even until death, that ye may be redeemed of God, and be numbered with those of the first resurrection, that ye may have eternal life. Now I say unto you, if this be the desire of your hearts, what have you against being baptized in the name of the Lord, as a witness before him that ye have entered into a covenant with him, that ye will serve him and keep his commandments, that he may pour out his Spirit more abundantly upon you? (Mosiah 18:8–10)*

Let's break this down into the three fundamental requirements of membership in the Church.

The first requirement is to want to be part of the community. Conversion begins with being "desirous to come into the fold of God, and to be called his people." This seems simple to us: of course someone would have to want to be part of the Church they are joining—duh! But the idea that an individual can just decide what religion to belong to is a very modern one in the Western world. From Constantine through Jefferson, Western Christianity was organized around state churches to which one belonged as a matter of national citizenship. Religious affiliation was not freely chosen, and, by the terms of Alma's baptismal covenant, ineffective.

One of the most important thing that we learn about the Nephite Church in subsequent chapters of the Book of Mormon is that, even when it becomes the official state religion, it adopts an official policy of religious toleration (Alma 30:7). This means that people can choose not to belong to the Church. But it also means that people who do belong to the Church have to choose the relationship affirmatively. If we look closely, we can see echoes of a powerful doctrine here: that religious affiliation must be entirely unconstrained—formally by the state or informally by family and cultural mechanisms such as guilt and shame—or it cannot count as "conversion."

The second requirement is to enter into a covenant with the other members of the community. The original baptismal covenant involved exactly 204 people. It is extremely important that the first covenant that they made was with each other, rather than with a formal organization. To qualify for membership in the *ekklesia*, they had to promise to "bear one another's burdens, that they may be light," to "mourn with those that mourn," and "to comfort those that stand in need of comfort." They had to promise, in other words, to become an integral part of the lives of 203 other people—and to learn to treat them as they would members of their own family.

The clear implication here is that learning how to love a few hundred other people is the most important thing that happens in the Church of Christ. "Conversion" doesn't mean to change religions, or even to become someone who thinks that Jesus is really neat. It means to give up the essential selfishness and tribalism of natural humanity and become capable of seeing and treating other people as Christ sees and treats them—which is also what Paul meant by the word that the KJV translates as "charity." An *ekklesia* is a school of Christlike love—a contained religious community where we can learn how to love actual people in the way that Christ requires of His disciples.

The third requirement is to "stand as witnesses of God at all times and in all things, and in all places that ye may be in, even until death." This is the core of discipleship—not allegiance to an institution or to a set of doctrines, but a willingness to testify constantly of the reality of Christ and the centrality of the atonement. This requirement of baptism comes with a powerful promise—"that ye may be redeemed of God, and be numbered with those of the first resurrection, that ye may have eternal life." It is the mutuality of these promises that makes them a covenant, and, through baptism, Alma's followers further covenanted to "serve him and keep his commandments that he may pour out his Spirit more abundantly upon you"—which is the commitment that we now renew each week by taking the sacrament.

It is no accident that "to stand as witnesses of God" is part of the same sentence as "comfort those who stand in need of comfort"; the former proceeds directly from the latter. For Alma, as for Paul, this is the defining characteristic of the *ekklesia*: it is a personal relationship with Christ that is part of—and inseparable from—relationships with the other members of a community.

To really get what Alma means here, I think, we need to change the way that we usually think about the Church. We are all used to thinking of "the Church" as a large international religious organization with 15 million members and an organized hierarchy with its corporate headquarters in Salt Lake City. But for both Paul and Alma, the Church, or the *ekklesia*, was almost entirely local. It had to be because we have to know actual people very well in order to love them meaningfully. It is easy to love everybody in the world theoretically. It is much harder to love Brother Jones, who takes 20 minutes each testimony meeting to explain about the Belgian Illuminati and the Antichrist. We learn to love in our wards and branches. When Alma says "church," this is what he means.

We live our lives as testaments of Christ to the extent that we learn to adopt His perspective on (among other things) other people. And we learn how to adopt such a perspective by serving, and being served by people whose lives we have allowed to intertwine with our own. For both Paul and Alma, religious conversion is less about accepting a set of orthodoxies and more about joining a community of believers whom we covenant to love and support as though they were members of our own family. This is not something that we have to do because we are disciples; it what being a disciple means.

# 19

## Nephites at War (Mainly with Themselves)

SO HERE'S A THING I DID: in order to lighten things up during all of the war chapters in the middle books of the Book of Mormon, I started trying to keep track of the wars. I figured that it would be fun to separate out all of the battle scenes into coherent sustained conflicts, like "New World War I," "New World War II," "the Zarahemla Police Action," and so forth. I hoped, in the end, to have something like a grand map of the Nephite-Lamanite conflicts in the Book of Mormon.

The problem is, there weren't any. When I finished, all of my notes ultimately said "Civil War." As I dredged through the blood and gore, I could not find a single sustained war between the Nephites and the Lamanites that was not actually an extension of some internecine Nephite conflict or another in which at least one party—and often both—found ways to involve the Lamanites on their side. Through some of the more sustained conflicts, a strong enough pattern emerges to justify calling it a type scene—an event or description that occurs in substantially the same form in multiple points in the text.

Here are four entries in what I will call the "Nephites-Involve-the-Lamanites-in-their-Civil-War" type scene. I hope that this analysis will push back on some of the ugliest racial stereotypes in the etiological narrative that the Book of Mormon was once believed to have been:

### Civil War I (Mosiah 23-24)

After the former Colony of Zeniff has fractured into several entities, Amulon, who had been one of the evil priests of King Noah, ingratiates himself with the King of the Lamanites. King Laman (for so is he called) allows Amulon to establish a client state within the Lamanite borders. Apparently, this is not the only Nephite satrapy in Lamaniteland; King Laman has made similar arrangements with two other cities called Shemlon and Shilom (Mosiah 24: 1–2), as well as with Helam, the city settled by Alma and the Church (Mosiah 23: 29).

Because Amulon was such a good ingratiater, Laman, the ingratiatee, appoints him a ruler over all of the other Nephites in the land, causing a period of great oppression in which Nephites persecute other Nephites using Lamanite muscle to do their dirty deeds:

> And now it came to pass that Amulon began to exercise
> authority over Alma and his brethren, and began to persecute
> him, and cause that his children should persecute their children.
> For Amulon knew Alma, that he had been one of the king's
> priests, and that it was he that believed the words of Abinadi
> and was driven out before the king, and therefore he was wroth

*with him; for he was subject to king Laman, yet he exercised*
*authority over them, and put tasks upon them, and put task-*
*masters over them. (Mosiah 24:8–9)*

This conflict ends happily, with Alma and the Church
sneaking out in the middle of the night and reuniting with the
Zarahemlans, but sets in place a pattern of Nephite-Lamanite
relations that continues throughout the middle books of the Book
of Mormon.

### Civil War II (Alma 2-4)

The major war in the first part of Alma starts in the fifth
year of the reign of the judges when a man named Amlici decides
that he wants to be the king. A lot of people agree, but he is
defeated at the polls. Nonetheless, his followers consecrate Amlici
the King of the Nephites (Alma 2:9). In the long civil war that
followed, the Amlicites are defeated, so (naturally) they go out in
the wilderness and form an alliance with the Lamanites, going
as far as to mark themselves in the same way that God marked
the Lamanites (Alma 3:18). When the Amlicites march back on
Zarahemla, their army is mingled with the Lamanites (Alma 3:20)
who have, in ways not fully explained by the text, been co-opted
in the service of one side of the Civil War.

### Civil War III, a.k.a. "The Big One" (Alma 45-62)

The Great Big War of the Book of Mormon takes up most
of Alma 45–62. This is the "Good War"—the one with all of the
great battles and heroes and villains and the Standard of Liberty

and Captain Moroni rallying men to the cause of freedom. And like most big wars, it was fought partially through propaganda that survives in Mormon's narrative. But the causes of the war are so similar to those of Civil War II (Alma 2–4) that it makes sense to read them together as type scenes, or narratives designed to be read together so that each can become a clarifying foil for the other.

The Big Nephite War starts when a man named Amalickiah decides that he wants to be the king. A lot of people agree, but he is defeated at the polls—with a lot of help from Captain Moroni and his torn clothing. Like Amlici, they go out into the wilderness and form an alliance with the Lamanites, but in this case we have a lot more information about how this alliance actually works out. Through treachery, poison, assassination, and general Machiavellian ickiness, Amalickiah becomes the King of the Lamanites (Alma 47), whom he leads against Captain Moroni and the Nephites—who conscript their own Lamanite army (the 2000 stripling warriors) in what is really another Nephite war about kingship and governance.

### Civil War IV (Helaman 11)

After the two Civil Wars in Alma—both caused by would-be kings forming alliances with the Lamanites—Mormon has a firmly established type scene to use in future conflicts. All he has to do is start to tell a fraction of the story, and we can piece together the rest. Here, for example, is a whole (and very similar) war contained in a single verse:

*And it came to pass that in the eightieth year of the reign of the judges over the people of Nephi, there were a certain number of the dissenters from the people of Nephi, who had some years before gone over unto the Lamanites, and taken upon themselves the name of Lamanites, and also a certain number who were real descendants of the Lamanites, being stirred up to anger by them, or by those dissenters, therefore they commenced a war with their brethren. (Helaman 11: 24)*

Mormon doesn't tell us more because he doesn't have to. We have seen this rodeo before. We have a pretty good idea how it started, and we can guess how it ended—such is the marvelous economy of the well-wrought type scene.

So, what's the big takeaway here? This is one more example of how the common reading of the Lamanites as a "wild, ferocious, and bloodthirsty" people doesn't hold up to a close reading of the text. This is the Nephite propaganda, much of which survives Mormon's redaction. But in all of the wars described in Mosiah, Alma, and Helaman, the Lamanites are bit players and mercenary soldiers in what are essentially conflicts between various groups of wild, ferocious, and bloodthirsty Nephites.

# 20

## Alma and the Poetics of Conversion

ONE OF THE TWENTIETH CENTURY'S GREATEST WORKS of Dante criticism is John Freccero's remarkable *Dante and the Poetics of Conversion*. Freccero makes two crucial points in this book: 1) that the primary objective of the Divine Comedy is to cause readers to experience conversion; and 2) that everything about the text—its subject matter, narrative style, linguistic manner, rhyme scheme, etc.—serves this greater objective. The purpose of Dante's work is to help readers both see and feel the experience of conversion.

I believe that we can say much the same thing about the Book of Mormon. On its very first page, it announces its own purpose as "to shew unto the remnant of the House of Israel how great things that Lord hath done for their fathers" and "to convinc[e] the Jew and Gentile that Jesus is the Christ." This work of conversion proceeds throughout the book until the very last chapter, which exhorts readers "to ask God, the Eternal Father, in the name of Christ, if these things are not true" (Moroni 10:4). It asks us, in other words, to both understand and experience conversion.

The stories of Alma and his descendants are central to the Book of Mormon's poetics of conversion. The story begins with Alma's dramatic conversion by Abinadi in the court of King Noah, and it moves through the next two generations of Alma's prophetic line to encompass almost every aspect of the conversion experience. And along the way, Mormon takes a number of unprecedented poetic steps to enhance this experience.

Alma's initial conversion is described in the sparsest of prose. After presenting the prophecies of Abinadi in great detail, without a hint that anybody is paying attention, Mormon tells us that "there was one among them whose name was Alma, he also being a descendant of Nephi." The rest of Mosiah largely tells the story of Alma's actions after being converted. He starts teaching other people, baptizes them, creates the first Nephite Church, and eventually relocates to Zarahemla to be the head of the Church in all the land.

I suspect that Mormon spends so little time describing the actual conversion, and so much time showing us what being converted looks like, because of the kind of conversion that Alma experiences. Like Saul in the New Testament, he is already a devoted follower of the truth as he understands it. His conversion, therefore, is primarily intellectual: Abinadi convinces him that the truth he understands is incorrect, or at least incomplete. Once he understands this he places his existing spiritual passion in the service of his new knowledge. It is the heavy lifting after conversion that we really need to see.

But this is not what conversion looks like for Alma's son. Alma the Younger grows up in his father's Church, and he makes a conscious decision to oppose it. The strong suggestion of the narrative is that Alma (like Nehor and Korihor, whose stories are interspersed with Alma the Younger's) actively chooses evil for evil's sake and intentionally opposes the Church that he knows to be true:

> *Now the sons of Mosiah were numbered among the unbelievers;*
> *and also one of the sons of Alma was numbered among them,*
> *he being called Alma, after his father; nevertheless, he became*
> *a very wicked and an idolatrous man. And he was a man*
> *of many words, and did speak much flattery to the people;*
> *therefore he led many of the people to do after the manner of his*
> *iniquities. And he became a great hindrement to the prosperity*
> *of the church of God; stealing away the hearts of the people;*
> *causing much dissension among the people; giving a chance for*
> *the enemy of God to exercise his power over them.* (Mosiah 27:
> 8–9)

As Mormon narrates Alma the Younger's conversion—once again invoking the New Testament account of Saul/Paul—he uses the plain and direct language of the historian to tell of angels, divine communication, paternal prayers, and some serious smiting—all of which Mormon describes with his typical historian's detachment. But then, in a remarkable moment of narrative conversion, Mormon pulls back and lets Alma take the mic:

> *My soul hath been redeemed*
> *from the gall of bitterness*

> *and bonds of iniquity.*
> *I was in the darkest abyss;*
> *but now I behold the marvelous light of God.*
> *My soul was racked with eternal torment;*
> *but I am snatched,*
> *and my soul is pained no more. (Mosiah 27:29)*

I follow Grant Hardy here in printing these lines in verse to emphasize that they are, in fact, poetry, complete with metaphor, elevated diction, and formal parallelism. The switch from prose to poetry, like the shift from the third- to the first-person point of view, highlights conversion, or change. This is precisely the sort of thing that Freccero meant by "the poetics of conversion."

But Mormon is not done with this conversion story. In one of very few examples of straight repetition in the Book of Mormon narrative, Mormon has Alma the Younger retell the story of his conversion to his son, Helaman, whom he is preparing to take over as the head of the Church. This time, the entire conversion narrative shifts to the first-person, and the brief poem at the end is expanded into a full-scale philosophical reflection on the nature of repentance:

> *I was racked with eternal torment, for my soul was harrowed*
> *up to the greatest degree and racked with all my sins. Yea, I did*
> *remember all my sins and iniquities, for which I was tormented*
> *with the pains of hell; yea, I saw that I had rebelled against my*
> *God, and that I had not kept his holy commandments. Yea,*
> *and I had murdered many of his children, or rather led them*

*away unto destruction; yea, and in fine so great had been my
iniquities, that the very thought of coming into the presence of
my God did rack my soul with inexpressible horror. Oh, thought
I, that I could be banished and become extinct both soul and
body, that I might not be brought to stand in the presence of my
God, to be judged of my deeds.*

*And now, for three days and for three nights was I racked,
even with the pains of a damned soul. And it came to pass that
as I was thus racked with torment, while I was harrowed up
by the memory of my many sins, behold, I remembered also to
have heard my father prophesy unto the people concerning the
coming of one Jesus Christ, a Son of God, to atone for the sins of
the world.*

*Now, as my mind caught hold upon this thought, I cried
within my heart: O Jesus, thou Son of God, have mercy on me,
who am in the gall of bitterness, and am encircled about by the
everlasting chains of death. And now, behold, when I thought
this, I could remember my pains no more; yea, I was harrowed
up by the memory of my sins no more. (Alma 36: 12–19)*

Here, Alma uses some of the most intense poetic language in
the entire Book of Mormon to describe the internal journey of
conversion. After experiencing irresistible and downright
intrusive grace, that saves him from the fate of Nehor and
Korihor (both of whose stories occur in between the two
conversion accounts), Alma experiences profound existential
despair. He actively wants to stop existing—to "be banished and
become extinct both soul and body." The final act of grace—and

the culmination of Alma the Younger's conversion—consists
of converting despair to hope. So important is the story of this
conversion that Mormon makes the unprecedented narrative
decision to tell it twice.

For the first Alma, conversion is a relatively simple affair.
He changes his mind, and all of the heavy lifted comes in living
a converted life. For his son, conversion is much more difficult
because it requires a change of heart and a painful process of
reconciliation with God. Like Dante, Mormon uses every literary
and narrative device at his disposal to let the reader see, feel,
and experience Alma the Younger's journey from deliberate sin,
through existential despair, to a state of divine hope in which he,
like Dante (and like the readers of both) can behold, once again,
the stars.

# 21

## Alma the Younger on the Road to Damascus: How the Book of Mormon Reads and Re-reads the Bible

THE BIBLE IS FULL OF TYPE SCENES that give a sense of narrative unity to its very diverse collection of texts. Type scenes can connect two characters within a single book, as the two "woman at the well" betrothal scenes in Genesis do. But they work their connective magic when they work across texts—and especially when they occur between the Old and New Testaments—consider the "King-Orders-the-Deaths-of-All-Male-Babies" scenes that begin both Exodus and Matthew. Such parallel scenes give a powerful boost to the argument that the Old and New Testaments testify of the same things.

Given the role that the Book of Mormon claims for itself as "Another Testament of Jesus Christ," we should not be surprised to find type scenes that connect its narrative to the other two Testaments. Indeed, we should be surprised, and a bit concerned, not to find them; fortunately, they are all over the place. We have already talked about the Tree of Life, Father's Blessing, and Olive Tree type scenes that connect the parts of the Book of Mormon to parts of the Bible—but these actually take some work to understand. We find a much more obvious example of the type scene in the conversion narratives of Saul (Acts 19 in the Bible) and Alma the Younger (Mosiah 27 in the Book of Mormon).

Both scenes are familiar enough that I don't need to paraphrase them here. Instead, I will briefly gloss the narrative elements that establish their structural similarity.

| Saul (Acts 9) | Alma the Younger (Mosiah 27) |
| --- | --- |
| Saul is well known for "breathing out threatenings and slaughter against the disciples of the Lord". (9:1) | Alma the Younger and his companions "became a great hinderment to the prosperity of the church of God; stealing away the hearts of the people; causing much dissension among the people". (27: 9) |
| He and his companions were stopped on their way to persecute Christians, "and suddenly there shined round about him a light from heaven". (9:3) | While they were persecuting the members of the Church, Alma and his companions (the Sons of Mosiah) saw an angel, who "descended as it were in a cloud". (27:11) |
| "He fell to the earth, and heard a voice saying unto him, Saul, Saul, why persecutest thou me?" (9:4) | The angel spoke to Alma and said, "arise and stand forth, for why persecutest thou the church of God?" (27: 13) |

| Saul (Acts 9) | Alma the Younger (Mosiah 27) |
|---|---|
| He is stricken with a physical disability and becomes unable to eat: "And he was three days without sight, and neither did eat nor drink". (9: 9) | He is stricken with a physical disability and becomes physically weak: "the astonishment of Alma was so great that he became dumb, that he could not open his mouth; yea, and he became weak, even that he could not move his hands; therefore he was taken by those that were with him, and carried helpless, even until he was laid before his father". (27: 19) |
| His blindness is healed, and he becomes able to eat, when he is converted to Christianity by Ananias. (9: 18–19) | His muteness is healed, and his body is strengthened, when he repents and is converted. (27:23) |
| Years later, he retells the story as a first-person narrative that is also included in the text. (Acts 22) | Years later, he retells the story as a first-person narrative that is also included in the text. (Alma 36) |

These elements are not identical—there is certainly a difference between the angel that Alma sees and the resurrected Christ that Paul sees. But they are too structurally similar to be the result of mere coincidence. Whatever the intentions of Alma (in telling) or Mormon (in redacting) this story, its appearance in a text published in 1830, in a Bible-saturated culture, must be read as a connection that somebody intended.

As with most stories that are mainly similar, however, it is the differences that really matter. Otherwise, we wouldn't need them both. And there are some key structural differences between

Paul's and Alma's conversion that we need to explore further to understand how the Book of Mormon adds value to the Bible:

| Saul | Alma the Younger |
| --- | --- |
| Saul is an elite member of his culture's established church persecuting an offshoot that he believes to be heretical. | Alma the Younger, the son of the head of his culture's established church, has become a leader in an offshoot that his father believes to be heretical. |
| Saul's persecution is physical. He acknowledges beating men and women in the synagogue and even persecuting them "unto death" (22: 4). | Alma's persecution is rhetorical. He confesses to "murdering" people, but then defines that as "led them away unto destruction" (Alma 36:14). His form of persecution was convincing people not to believe in Christ. |
| Saul was a deeply religious person who (according to the text) believed in the wrong religion. He had to change his beliefs. | Alma was a person raised in the true church who, out of wickedness, set about to destroy people's faith. He had to change his behavior. |
| Saul is converted because the Lord needs him for a very specific purpose, as He tells Ananias: "He is a chosen vessel unto me, to bear my name before the Gentiles, and kings, and the children of Israel". (Acts 9:15) | Alma is converted because of the prayers of his father. The angel tells him specifically, "I come to convince thee of the power and authority of God, that the prayers of his servants might be answered according to their faith". (Mosiah 27:14) |

Taken together, the two narratives show us how God intervenes for very different reasons to change the lives of two different kinds of people who are guilty of different kinds of sins. Despite very different starting positions, however, Alma the Younger and Saul end up having almost exactly the same conversion experience with exactly the same results. The two narratives, in this case, encourage us to universalize the possibility of conversion—to remove the possibility of context-specific interpretations and understand that real, meaningful change is ALWAYS possible for us and for those we love.

Perhaps the most important similarity between Alma the Younger and Saul, though, is that neither of them deserve the blessings they get. They did nothing to merit the miraculous divine interventions that changed them in fundamental ways. They were surprised by grace for reasons that they could never have understood or expected. This, it turns out, is how it always works.

# 22

## Nephites and Judges and Kings (Oh My)

AT THE END OF THE BOOK OF MOSIAH, the Nephite's
governmental structure changes from kings to judges, bringing
a full circle to the transition from judges to kings that occurred
nearly a thousand years earlier in Israel (1 Samuel 8–11). In a
very real way, the Book of Mormon walks back one of the most
controversial political passages in the entire Bible—and it does so
through a process of almost complete narrative inversion.

In 1 Samuel, the Deuteronomic historian describes the end of
the rule of the judges (who were more like military heroes than
judicial figures). Samuel the prophet appoints his sons "judges
over Israel" (8:1), but the people rebel. Samuel's sons are corrupt,
they complain, and besides, all of the cool countries have kings.
They go to Samuel and demand a king too. In what would one day
become one of the most contested political pronouncements in
the Bible, Samuel explains to them why they shouldn't want any
such thing:

> *And he said, this will be the manner of the king that shall
> reign over you: He will take your sons, and appoint them for*

*himself, for his chariots, and to be his horsemen; and some shall run before his chariots. And he will appoint him captains over thousands, and captains over fifties; and will set them to ear his ground, and to reap his harvest, and to make his instruments of war, and instruments of his chariots.*

*And he will take your daughters to be confectionaries, and to be cooks, and to be bakers. And he will take your fields, and your vineyards, and your oliveyards, even the best of them, and give them to his servants. And he will take the tenth of your seed, and of your vineyards, and give to his officers, and to his servants.*

*And he will take your menservants, and your maidservants, and your goodliest young men, and your asses, and put them to his work. He will take the tenth of your sheep: and ye shall be his servants. And ye shall cry out in that day because of your king which ye shall have chosen you; and the LORD will not hear you in that day.* (1 Samuel 8:11–18)

This passage became enormously controversial in England (and much of Europe) during the 17th century, or the "Century of Revolution," when it was used to define the doctrine of the Divine Right of Kings. No less a figure than King James I (the Bible Guy) staked the absolutist claims of the Stuarts on this very passage—claiming that Samuel's parade of horribles represents the legitimate power of a monarch, accepted by the people and endorsed by the voice of God. In this opinion he was backed by, among others, Robert Filmer, Thomas Hobbes, and the not-

very-famous-anymore poet Abraham Cowley, whose epic poem
*Davideis* was considered the last word on the subject.

Oliver Cromwell and that lot disagreed, as did John Locke,
Daniel Defoe, the Earl of Shaftesbury, and the late-century
political faction that became known as the "Whigs." Whiggism
advanced the interpretation that eventually won the day, which
is that God told Samuel how bad kings would be because, for the
most part, kings were bad—or at least potentially scary enough
that they should be kept on a very short leash.

All of this seventeenth-century history became important
to the nineteenth-century context of the Book of Mormon
when Andrew Jackson was elected president in 1828. Soon after
Jackson's election, Henry Clay and his political allies formed the
National Republican Party (as opposed to Jackson's Democratic-
Republican Party), which very soon came to be known as the
"Whigs" because they opposed the tyranny of Andrew Jackson.
This was roughly the political situation when Joseph Smith first
published the Book of Mormon. Jackson was wildly popular with
people who had not been part of the political class before, but
he was also held in deep suspicion by the political elite (think:
Donald Trump) as an unpredictable character who could start
America down the road to tyranny.

This is why it would have been significant to readers in 1830—
when all of this poop was in the process of hitting the fan—that
the Nephite monarchy dissolves into a reign of judges that
continues until the coming of Christ. Not only does this highlight
a contemporary argument—it revises and reinterprets the very
biblical passage at the heart of that controversy. In a complete

inversion of Samuel, who appointed his sons to be judges, Mosiah offers the kingdom to his sons and is refused. Rather than risk a new hereditary monarchy, he warns the people about kings using rhetoric very similar to Samuel's rhetoric a thousand years earlier:

> Behold, O ye my people, or my brethren, for I esteem you as such, I desire that ye should consider the cause which ye are called to consider—for ye are desirous to have a king. Now I declare unto you that he to whom the kingdom doth rightly belong has declined, and will not take upon him the kingdom. And now if there should be another appointed in his stead, behold I fear there would rise contentions among you. And who knoweth but what my son, to whom the kingdom doth belong, should turn to be angry and draw away a part of this people after him, which would cause wars and contentions among you, which would be the cause of shedding much blood and perverting the way of the Lord, yea, and destroy the souls of many people. (Mosiah 29: 6–7)

And thus the reign of the judges begins, as if King Mosiah had corrected the mistake that the people of Israel made a thousand years ago and returned power to the people through the mechanism of the judges—like any good Jacksonian American would have done in the same situation.

But in context it is not quite so easy, as the judges don't do any better than the kings would have. As the Books of Alma and Helaman progress, it becomes clear that judges are just as capable of "perverting the way of the Lord" as kings ever were. Like the reigns of David and Solomon, the reigns of Benjamin and Mosiah become a sort of golden age for the generations that follow.

Though the Book of Mormon inverts the Bible's transition from judges to monarchy, it ends up teaching about the same lesson that the Hebrew narrative does—which is that every form of government outside of the Kingdom of God has, not only problems, but fatal flaws that will ultimately destroy it. This would have been a cynical buzzkill to Americans high on Jacksonian optimism, but, as the Latter-day Saints would soon discover, "government by the people" has plenty of fatal flaws. Ultimately, both the Bible and the Book of Mormon end up teaching us that people usually end up with the government they deserve, which may be the most depressing thing I have ever known.

# 23

## Nehor's Universalism Problem—and Ours

SHEREM, NEHOR, AND KORIHOR—Mormon scripture's three
most famous anti-Christs—constitute one of the most obvious
recurring type-scenes in the Book of Mormon. Of the three, the
middle child, Nehor, is clearly the most disruptive. Long after
he receives the just desserts traditional for his ilk (Alma 1: 15),
Nehorism pops up as the principle religion of most of the other
bad guys in the Book of Alma (see Alma 14:4–8, Alma 21:4, Alma
24:28). Only Gadianton can claim a similarly evil influence on the
Nephite people.

But there is a huge difference between the signature heresies
of Nehor and those of Gadianton. The latter taught that it was
possible to murder and get gain—hardly an original insight in the
world, but an extremely disruptive one nonetheless.

Nehor, on the other hand, taught that:

*All mankind should be saved at the last day, and that they need
not fear nor tremble, but that they might lift up their heads and
rejoice; for the Lord had created all men, and had also redeemed*

*all men; and, in the end, all men should have eternal life
(Alma 1:9).*

Nineteenth century readers would have had no trouble
identifying Nehor's religion: he was a Universalist, or a believer in
universal salvation. Before Mormonism came along, Universalism
was the most controversial religion in the New World. Emerging
from several Pietist sects in the 18th century, American
Universalism consolidated into a coherent religious organization
in a General Convention held in Winchester, New Hampshire, in
1805. The convention adopted three articles of faith:

- We believe that the Holy Scripture of the Old and New
  Testaments contain a revelation of the character of
  God and of the duty, interest, and final destination of
  mankind.
- We believe that there is one God whose nature is Love,
  revealed in one Lord, Jesus Christ by one Holy Spirit
  of grace, who will finally restore the whole family of
  mankind to holiness and happiness.
- We believe that holiness and true happiness are
  inseparably connected, and that believers ought to be
  careful to maintain order and practise good works; for
  these things are good and profitable unto men.

By 1830, the Universalist Church was among the largest
denominations in the country. Throughout the 19th century, its
famous membership would include Judith Sargent Murray, Clara

Barton, P.T. Barnum, Olympia Browne, and Joseph Smith, Senior, the father of the Mormon prophet, whose own father was the co-founder of a Universalist society in Vermont.

But Universalism was almost as controversial on the American frontier as Mormonism. The doctrine of universal salvation was roundly criticized by Catholics, who believed that baptism is required for salvation, and by most Protestants, who believed that those who did not believe in or follow Christ would be damned to the biblical hell. But the strongest rejection came from the moral pragmatists, who argued that the idea of hell is necessary to keep people from doing bad stuff. Pretty much everybody hated the Universalists.

Including, it seems, the Nephite Church. Through Nehor, the Book of Mormon condemns Universalism in terms that most nineteenth-century Christians would immediately recognize. Nehor preaches the standard 19th-century Universalist shtick and, as if to prove that Universalism is a slippery slope to murder (because, hey, why should anyone refrain from killing people if there is no hell to burn in for all of eternity), kills a popular Nephite hero named Gideon who tries to stop him.

To the person reading the Book of Mormon as a 19th century document, none of this should be surprising. The Book of Mormon presents Protestant party line on a lot of things like heaven, hell, and salvation. The surprise comes later on, during the Nauvoo period, when Joseph Smith develops a theology that any nineteenth-century Catholic or Protestant would describe as Universalist.

Two specific innovations from the Nauvoo period move Latter-day Saint theology into the Universalist camp.

The doctrine of vicarious baptism universalizes baptism by ensuring that it is performed on behalf of every human being who has ever lived. Thus, Latter-day Saints can insist, as Catholics do, that baptism is required for salvation while still making the ordinance available to those who die without it. The ordinance ceases to filter souls into heaven and hell.

The doctrine of the Three Kingdoms of Glory eliminates the concept of hell altogether, neutralizing the eternal threat that "salvation" is supposed to save people from. Latter-day Saints do not believe in hell, only in three different flavors of heaven (as others understand it) which we can roughly describe as good, better, and best.

Though these doctrines do not constitute a theology of universal salvation from within the Mormon world view (since not everybody achieves the pinnacle of exaltation), they very clearly do constitute Universalism from any other Catholic or Protestant perspective: nobody goes to hell, everybody is resurrected physically, and God gives everybody the exact degree of spiritual glory that they can bear. We all get to be as happy as God can make us for all of eternity. [1]

And this is our Universalism problem. It is not that we are Universalists—I couldn't be happier about that one. Rather it is that, as is also the case with polygamy, the theology of the Book of Mormon conflicts with the current theology of the LDS Church. This is not really a problem. The whole point of having "living prophets" is that they can periodically announce new things that we have always believed. But it does mean that contemporary Latter-day Saints should be careful about how they use the Book of Mormon in conjunction with terms like "heaven," "hell," and "salvation"—since these are unstable ideas in Mormon scripture and practice.

## Endnotes

1.  Yes, I know that Mormons believe in "outer darkness" for a particular brand of sinner—the Denier of the Holy Ghost—but I am treating this as an outlier, since it does not appear to be even a possibility for most people. I am also aware that Nehor claims that all men shall have "eternal life", which contemporary Mormons define as exaltation in the Celestial Kingdom, but there is nothing in the text to suggest that either Nehor or the Nephites were aware of this concept when Nehor was speaking.

# 24

## Is Disagreement Always Rebellion?
## The Book of Mormon Anti-Christs and the
## Possibility of Sincere Religious Dissent

THE THREE MAJOR BOOK OF MORMON ANTI-CHRISTS—
Sherem, Nehor, and Korihor—are all instances of a single type-
scene, which means that they follow a similar narrative arc, which
is more important to the text than any one of their individual
stories.

The type scene goes like this: a charismatic teacher appears on
the scene preaching that Christ will not come. He develops a large
following and comes to the attention of the head of the Church,
who refutes his arguments with clear and compelling logic. The
anti-Christ ignores the overwhelming evidence and persists in his
false beliefs, which lead to an untimely and ignominious death.
But before he dies, he confesses that he always knew that his
teachings were false; it was just something the devil made him do.

Taken together, these three stories construct a version of
religious dissent that leaves very little room for sincere disbelief.
Their disagreements with the established Church have nothing to
do with their actually believing stuff—which could certainly not

have withstood the rhetorical assaults of Jacob and Alma. Rather, the sin of all three anti-Christs is rebellion against what they know perfectly well to be true.

We find this view of dissent throughout the Book of Mormon, beginning with Laman and Lemuel, who rebel against God despite seeing angels and miracles enough to convince anybody of His power and glory. And it continues on through Moroni's famous promise (Moroni 10:4), which says, in effect, that God will demonstrate the truth of the Book of Mormon to anybody who asks about it sincerely—a formulation that also means that anybody who does not receive a witness of the truth must not be sincere. In both its sermons and its narratives, the Book of Mormon tries very hard to close the door on the possibility of sincere dissent and frame all disagreement as willful disobedience against God.

But here's the thing: the door won't stay closed. Nowhere does the text of the Book of Mormon undercut its own rhetoric more than in its handling of the supposed deathbed confessions of the anti-Christs. Let's listen closely to Mormon as he narrates the last moments of Nehor's life:

> And it came to pass that they took him; and his name was Nehor; and they carried him upon the top of the hill Manti, and there he was caused, or rather did acknowledge, between the heavens and the earth, that what he had taught to the people was contrary to the word of God; and there he suffered an ignominious death. (Alma 1: 15)

Did you catch it? The text actually starts to say that Nehor was forced to admit that his beliefs were insincere, and then the narrator corrects himself (because it's hard to erase engraved hieroglyphics) to reframe it as a voluntary admission of guilt.

In context, though, the coerced confession that Mormon starts to tell us about makes much more sense. Nehor's views had become popular. The Church that he started plays an important role in Alma—and his followers include Amlici, Amalikiah, Korihor, and most of the Zoramite population. It is unlikely that a clearly confessed fraud would have inspired such a lasting movement. It seems much more likely that the state church in Zarahemla did what religious majorities have done to popular heretics for thousands of years—used torture to secure a confession in the hopes of discrediting the dissident views.

We get a tiny glimpse of something similar in Korihor's confession. Even though Korihor has not broken any law (there being at least the façade of religious freedom among the Nephites), he is bound in chains in Gideon and brought, by the civil authorities, to face the head of the Church. After demanding a sign of God's power from Alma and being struck dumb, Korihor writes out a complete (and, for Alma, extremely convenient) confession, acknowledging that he knew all along that he was deceiving the people (keep in mind that Korihor had just been subjected to a grievous physical injury that he was hoping to get reversed):

*Now the knowledge of what had happened unto Korihor*
*was immediately published throughout all the land; yea, the*

*proclamation was sent forth by the chief judge to all the people
in the land, declaring unto those who had believed in the
words of Korihor that they must speedily repent, lest the same
judgments would come unto them. (Alma 30: 57)*

What I find most interesting here is the speed with which Alma
and Nephihah distributed the confession. It was **immediately**
published throughout the land. This tells us that they needed the
confession because Korihor's followers were becoming disruptive
to both Church and State. And the cheery conclusion in verse
58—that his followers "were all converted again unto the Lord"—
is dramatically undercut by the rest of Alma, which narrates a
cataclysmic civil war between the Christians and the followers of
Nehor/Korihor. Mormon's continued assertion that these beliefs
are insincere becomes less and less plausible the more that people
demonstrate their willingness to die for them.

The entire Book of Mormon leaves very little room for honest
disbelief. Sincere dissent would complicate the whole narrative,
which works very hard to convince us that such a thing cannot
exist. But the text cannot pull it off. It keeps undercutting its own
attempts to portray religious dissent as willful rebellion. Traces of
sincere disagreement remain around the edges where the text has
tried to erase them—suggesting that conversion may have been
then, as it is now, a more difficult process than anybody wants to
admit or acknowledge.

# 25

## Religious Liberty and Persecution in the Era of Nephite Privilege

> And it came to pass that Alma was appointed to be the first chief judge, he being also the high priest, his father having conferred the office upon him, and having given him the charge concerning all the affairs of the church.

—Mosiah 29:42

THERE IS A BIG DIFFERENCE between "religious freedom" and "religious tolerance." Religious freedom derives from a society's belief that human beings have a natural right to their own belief systems and that, as James Madison puts it, "in matters of Religion, no man's right is abridged by the institution of Civil Society and that Religion is wholly exempt from its cognizance."

Religious tolerance, on the other hand, derives from the will and pleasure of the state. A society with religious tolerance endorses one set of religious beliefs over all others, but it allows other beliefs to exist on terms that it sets itself (and can revoke at any time). Religious dissent in such a society is seen, not as a natural right of all human beings, but as a civil right protected by the indulgence of the state—which officially disagrees but has a big enough heart to let you be wrong and go to hell in your own way.

The lines between religious liberty and religious tolerance often blur, but here is a quick and infallible test to determine the difference: if the official head of the government is also the official head of a state church, then you don't have actual religious liberty. The best you can hope for is tolerance—and probably not much of that either.

We should keep this in mind when reading the first few chapters of Alma. At the end of the previous book, both Mosiah the king, and Alma the head of the Church, go the way of all flesh. Alma the Younger becomes BOTH the head of Church and the first Chief Judge of the land. And yet, we are told, that "the law could have no power on any man for his belief" (Alma 1:17). There is something like religious freedom in Zarahemla, though it looks a lot like a weak and tepid religious tolerance.

The events of Alma 1 put this religious toleration—and the narrative that Mormon constructs around it—to a severe test. Alma's first challenge as prophet/chief judge comes when Nehor, a popular religious dissident, starts his own Church based on the twin pillars of universal salvation and a well-paid clergy. Nehor also commits a murder, making him fairly easy for Alma to dispatch, but the Church of Nehor remains to cause problems for Alma in both his religious and his political roles:

*Nevertheless, this did not put an end to the spreading of priestcraft through the land; for there were many who loved the vain things of the world, and they went forth preaching false doctrines; and this they did for the sake of riches and honor. Nevertheless, they durst not lie, if it were known, for fear of the law, for liars were punished; therefore they pretended to preach according to their belief; and now the law could have no power on any man for his belief. (Alma 1:16–17)*

We need to pay a lot of attention to these words and how they frame religious dissent in the Book of Mormon. And the first thing that we need to realize is that Mormon, the presumed narrator of this passage, is guessing at motivations that no historian working 500 years later could possibly know. Not only does he state that the doctrines of the Nehors are false; he asserts that those preaching the doctrines knew them to be false and only "pretended to preach according to their belief" so that they could not be prosecuted under the law.

Now, one may agree or disagree with having a paid clergy, or believing that God ultimately saves everybody, but these are beliefs that one can hold in good faith. Being wrong is not the same thing as being insincere, and historians never have sufficient access to the hearts and souls of their subjects to make these kinds of sweeping claims about whole categories of people in the past. If I were reading a history of Utah and came across a passage that read, "the first generation of Mormons in Utah pretended to believe that polygamy was necessary for salvation so that they could have sex with multiple women" I would know that I was in the presence of anti-Mormon propaganda.

And the narrative goes even further. Not only did the Nehors lie about what they believed; they also "began to persecute those that did belong to the Church of God, and had taken upon them the name of Christ." And what did this persecution consist of? They did "afflict them with all manner of words" (Alma 1:19–20).

We've really got to apply our context filters here. In the current and previous chapters we learn that the head of government in Zarahemla is also the chief prophet of the Church. The religious leadership therefore controls all of the coercive apparatuses of the state, and there is a law against persecuting Christians (yet apparently no law against persecuting anybody else). And we know that all of these things have been decided by a vote of the majority of the people. And yet the text asks us to believe that these same Christians are being persecuted when somebody speaks harsh words against them. This is precisely what it looks like when a powerful majority exercises its privileges.

And this should not surprise us at all. This is the difference between a society that recognizes universal human rights and one that begrudgingly accords limited privileges to those outside of the majority. In such societies—and I would certainly count our own here—the privileged majority almost always claims that they are being persecuted when they are being asked to apply the same standards to themselves that they inherently apply to everybody else. In the echo chambers of talk radio and online comments sections, no human being has ever been as oppressed as the straight, white, American male in the 21st century—you know, the guys who have all of the money and most of the power in the world.

If we accept the text's arguments in Alma 1, we must see the Christian Nephites in similar terms: they are the possessors of unique truth who are horribly oppressed by liars and thieves who knowingly teach false doctrines because they hate God and want to destroy the State. If we reject these assumptions, or even bracket them for just a moment, we might see something that looks a lot more like a bunch of highly privileged Nephites being certain that God is on their side and wielding that certainty as a club in order to protect their privileges.

It is certainly no coincidence that this is precisely the view of the Nephite Church that Alma will find when he gives up his civil power and tours the kingdom as a prophet of God.

# 26

## The Amlicite Revolution and the Problem of Religious Majoritarianism

THE STORY OF THE GREAT AMLICITE WAR in Alma 2–3 is a good example of how winners write history. Mormon's account of the event could not make the Amlicites look worse: they tried to overthrow the new system of judges but were defeated at the polls; they rebelled against the state; they joined the Lamanites and marked their own foreheads; they caused the needless death of thousands of people; and they were ultimately defeated because God was on the side of the Nephites.

Underneath Mormon's narrative there is a different and more disturbing story that explains the actions of the Amlicites and casts some light on the failure of the United States in one of its most recent military ventures. It is the story of religious majoritarianism.

Consider the following facts, all of which we can derive fairly easily from the text, but which I am going to spin slightly towards the perspective of the traditional bad guys:

- After the death of King Mosiah, the Nephite monarchy is replaced by a system of popularly elected judges. In practice, however, the chief judge functions very much like a king. In many cases, the office is even passed from father to son (or brother to brother) in what amounts to de-facto patrilineal succession.
- The first chief judge is also the head of the Church of Christ—which is founded on the (let's face it, rather odd) belief that, at some time in the future, a Jewish man with a Latin name will be born to a virgin and will die in a manner that will somehow allow us to repent for our sins. To be saved, we must call upon this Jewish/Roman man's name as though he had already lived and ask him to forgive us for the bad stuff we have already done.
- The Nephite Christians have a solid electoral majority and can therefore rubber-stamp the will of the Church in the political sphere—which guarantees that the coercive mechanisms of the state will always be at the service of the Church and its agendas.
- In Alma 1, a man named Nehor forms a dissenting religious sect that attracts many followers and creates a viable alternative to the established Church.
- Nehor is accused of killing a beloved Christian hero and forced to recant his beliefs before being executed in a public and deeply humiliating way clearly designed to discourage his followers.
- The official state Church brands the Nehors as heretics and coins the term "priestcraft" to describe their beliefs.

They pass a law against non-Christians criticizing
Christians, but they do not apply this law equally to
themselves. They increase their state-sanctioned criticism
of Nehor's church.

- The followers of Nehor band together under Amlici, who
runs against Alma in a public election.

- Amlici loses the election, as he must, because the
Christians have an electoral majority and, therefore, a
lock on "the voice of the people."

- Amlici's followers—the non-Christian population of
Zarahemla—reject Alma's leadership and start a
rebellion.

The story as I have told it is a very common one. As appealing as
it sounds to take every issue to "the voice of the people,"
this approach does not work very well when a single faction
controls a permanent majority. This problem—the problem of
majoritarianism—is the subject of Madison's Federalist #10, one
of the most important political essays ever written. A permanent
majority, Madison argues, undermines the basis of the democratic
process by creating a political entity capable of every bit as much
oppression as a king or a tyrant. Members of the permanent
minority rarely stay committed to a competitive political process
in which they can never win. They pull out, secede, or rebel.

Americans saw this dynamic clearly in their country's recent
military adventures in Iraq—a country in which the Shia religious
majority controls 55–60% of the vote, guaranteeing that the
minority Sunni population will always lose national elections. In
such a situation, the representative democracy that we tried to

create is a non-starter. The minority population has no reason to invest in a political process that will always work against them. Rather, they flock to those entities that promise them the political power they can never have in a lopsided democracy. Amlici was one such entity. The Islamic State was another.

During the Nephite Reign of the Judges, "the voice of the people" appears to have functioned as the ultimate form of political legitimation. That which was done by the voice of the people was right, and that which went against the voice of the people was wrong. This is an appealing notion to anyone who happens to be in a permanent majority. But it is as scary as hell to those in the minority, whose life and well-being must be constantly in the hands of people who too often perceive them as the enemy.

# 27

## A Mighty Change of Heart

BOTH RHETORICALLY AND TYPOLOGICALLY, Alma the Younger occupies the same space in the Book of Mormon that Paul occupies in the New Testament. The typological similarity begins with their conversion stories, which share so many structural elements that they can plausibly be considered variations of the same basic narrative.

After their conversions, the two men continue along similar trajectories. Alma gives up the Chief Judgeship and travels throughout the land, visiting the Churches that his father had set up. Paul goes on multiple journeys to set up and visit the Churches of Asia Minor. They both encounter congregations that have become divided and fractious—thereby implicitly rejecting the baptismal covenant to be united in faith. Both Alma and Paul make it clear that followers of Christ must do better.

Alma begins his journey in Zarahemla, the capital that he once governed, with the masterful sermon that takes up most of Alma 5. Significantly, Mormon steps out of the narrative and lets Alma speak for himself, without the editorial commentary so prominent in earlier chapters. The sermon is fairly long but extremely focused, and we can study it profitably in two parts. In the first part, Alma preaches repentance to the people, telling them that Christian salvation requires a "mighty change of heart." In the second part, Alma tells the people exactly what about their hearts needs to change.

Some variation of the phrase "mighty change of heart" appears five times in Alma 5:

- Verse 7: "Behold he [God] changed their hearts; yeah, he awakened them out of a deep sleep, and they awoke unto God."
- Verse 12: "And according to his [Alma the Elder's] faith there was a mighty change wrought in his heart."
- Verse 13 "And behold, he preached the word unto your fathers, and a mighty change was also wrought in their hearts."
- Verse 14: "And now behold, I ask of you, my brethren of the church, have ye spiritually been born of God? Have ye received his image in your countenances? Have ye experienced this mighty change in your hearts?"
- Verse 26: "And now behold, I say unto you, my brethren, if ye have experienced a change of heart, and if ye have felt to sing the song of redeeming love, I would ask, can ye feel so now?"

This is important. The mighty change of heart is one of the most rhetorically powerful phrases in the Book of Mormon. It clarifies the meaning of repentance, which is not a rote process of asking

God to pardon our sins by saying we're sorry and promising not to do them anymore. Repentance is the process by which we plead with God to change our nature—to make us different kinds of people than we were before.

Left here, Alma's discourse on repentance would be too abstract to help us much in actual practice. But Alma does not leave things here. After explaining that repentance is "a mighty change" from one kind of heart to another, Alma goes on to explain in detail what it is about our hearts that we have to change mightily:

> 53 And now my beloved brethren, I say unto you, can ye withstand these sayings; yea, can ye lay aside these things, and trample the Holy One under your feet; yea, can ye be puffed up in the pride of your hearts; yea, will ye still persist in the wearing of costly apparel and setting your hearts upon the vain things of the world, upon your riches? 54 Yea, will ye persist in supposing that ye are better one than another; yea, will ye persist in the persecution of your brethren, who humble themselves and do walk after the holy order of God, wherewith they have been brought into this church, having been sanctified by the Holy Spirit, and they do bring forth works which are meet for repentance—55 Yea, and will you persist in turning your backs upon the poor, and the needy, and in withholding your substance from them?

For Alma, these are the signs of apostasy: setting one's heart upon riches and displaying wealth, considering oneself better than others, and refusing to acknowledge or aid the poor and the needy. These are crimes against the Body of Christ. And they are implicit rejections of the covenants made by the first converts at the Waters of Mormon.

And we can group these sins together easily under the general heading of "selfishness," which is the natural state of humankind. We are frightened little mammals with an overpowering urge—built into us by millions of years of evolution—to act always in ways that favor our own interests and those of our offspring. The mighty change of heart that Alma speaks of is the mechanism by which God converts us from natural and selfish human beings to divine and selfless disciples of Christ. And the *ekklesia*—the body of fellow travelers with whom we interact regularly—is the school in which we learn how to love beyond our genetic best interests.

Alma, like Paul, knew well what a mighty change of heart looked like. Both men experienced dramatic conversions that set the stage for their life's ministries. Alma, though, had an even greater change to make when he became both the head of the Church and the Chief Judge of the land. One way to read Alma's Zarahemla Sermon is as an explanation of why he gave up the Chief Judgeship and set out to repair the Church.

As the head of both Church and State, Alma was easily the most powerful and influential person in the country. But, as the first four chapters of Alma show us, he did not do either job very well because they kept interfering with each other. His country was embroiled in a civil war for most of his tenure as Chief Judge—a war that he may well have caused by blurring the lines between his two positions and treating a religious rival as an enemy of the state.

In the meantime, nobody was looking after the Church as its congregations fell deeper and deeper into the forms of apostasy outlined above. I think it very likely that Alma's closing parable is aimed as much at himself as his audience:

> [59] *For what shepherd is there among you having many sheep doth not watch over them, that the wolves enter not and devour his flock? And behold, if a wolf enter his flock doth he not drive him out? Yea, and at the last, if he can, he will destroy him.*

Tending to his flock required Alma to give up his political position and all of its accompanying honors, pomp, and circumstance. It required him to do what Paul would do 200 years later and dedicate his life to setting the Church in order—without the power of the state, which he once commanded, at his back. This conversion was just as difficult and consequential as the one brought about by angelic fiat in his youth. It was a mighty change of heart that would have important consequences for the Church in his generation.

# 28

## Alma in Ammonihah

IMAGINE THAT, DURING THE TWILIGHT of his second term, Barack Obama resigned from office in order to travel through the Red States preaching the virtue of medicare expansion. Imagine further that he decided to start in Utah, the most Republican state in the union, which voted 3–1 for his opponent in 2012. Given Utah's religious population, Obama might feel that he could convince people that caring for the poor is a Christian duty. He could quote Jesus and, if he did some advance reading, King Benjamin. How do you think this would go down?

Yeah, a complete train wreck, right?

This is more or less what Alma did when he went to Ammonihah. As the head of both Church and State, Alma was deeply involved in the Amlicite Civil War, which pitted the majority Christians against the minority of the population that did not belong to the Church. We soon discover that Ammonihah is a Nehorite stronghold that would have opposed Alma bitterly during the recent war. When Alma shows up in their town square, then, the people treat him like a political enemy who no longer has the power to hurt them:

*Nevertheless, they hardened their hearts, saying unto him: Behold, we know that thou art Alma; and we know that thou art high priest over the church which thou hast established in many parts of the land, according to your tradition; and we are not of thy church, and we do not believe in such foolish traditions. And now we know that because we are not of thy church we know that thou hast no power over us; and thou hast delivered up the judgment-seat unto Nephihah; therefore thou art not the chief judge over us. (Alma 8: 11–12)*

We must remember here that this is both a religious and a political dispute. Religious affiliation is the major dividing line of this society, and Alma's tenure as the combined head of both church and state had disastrous consequences. Alma cannot separate his religious message from its political connotations in a country that is sharply divided along religious lines. What's more, he doesn't even try. Rather, he makes it clear that the problems of Ammonihah have more to do with politics than theology:

*And now behold, I say unto you, that the foundation of the destruction of this people is beginning to be laid by the unrighteousness of your lawyers and your judges. And now it came to pass that when Amulek had spoken these words the people cried out against him, saying: Now we know that this man is a child of the devil, for he hath lied unto us; for he hath spoken against our law. And now he says that he has not spoken against it. And again, he has reviled against our lawyers, and our judges. (Alma 10:27–29)*

Keep in mind that "judges" are executive officials in this context, so Alma is criticizing the political elite and saying that Ammonihah has incurred divine disfavor because of the behavior of its leaders, who (unlike the kings of the Bible) have been elected by the "voice of the people." He gives very few specifics, other than referring to general wickedness and rehearsing his theological arguments against Nehorian universalism. The Ammonihah section focuses primarily on the theological disputes, but the text makes it clear that it is not Alma's theology that whips everybody into a frenzy, but his politics.

We have to consider both the theological and the political aspects of Alma's mission to understand some of the most disturbing aspects of this section. Alma and Amulek dispute in the public square with Zeezrom and the other lawyers, and they make some converts among the women and children. These converts are then burned alive before their eyes (Alma 14: 8). This seems like a horrific punishment for changing religions in a country that supposedly has religious freedom. But it was also the ancient world's most common penalty for treason against the state.

After seeing their converts burned alive, Alma and Amulek are arrested, imprisoned, and questioned by "many lawyers, and judges, and priests, and teachers, who were of the profession of Nehor" (14: 18). The political elite of Ammonihah ask them derisively, "Will ye stand again and judge this people, and condemn our law" (14:20), making it very clear that they construe Alma's theological positions as political attacks. They keep Alma and Amulek in prison, naked, bound by strong chords, and deprived of food and water—which would have ensured their gruesome deaths had God not finally stepped in and rent stuff in twain.

This seems like a horrible and gruesome way to treat a couple of sincere missionaries who are only trying to save people's souls and keep God from smiting their town. It makes much more sense, however, when we consider it part of the multi-generational conflict between the Nehors and the Christians that, in one form or another, takes up the entire Book of Alma. We will miss a lot of important stuff if we read this as only a religious division. Like Catholics and Protestants in Reformation Wars, and like Sunni and Shia Muslims in Iraq today, the Christians and the Nehors were permanent religious factions that divided society in the Book of Alma.

This massive confusion between church and state in Nephiteland should not surprise us one bit. Human societies have always worked this way. Human beings have never drawn clear lines between religious virtue (what I should choose to do) and political virtue (what everybody should be compelled to do). We are not wired to think this way. We see virtue as virtue, good as good, and bad as bad—and we generally think that the laws of the state should see things the same way. Separation of church and state is a very recent innovation in the world, and nobody is very good at it yet.

So let's go back to Obama arguing in Utah that the Christian imperative to care for the poor should make us want to expand Medicaid. Good conservatives would certainly counter that Jesus never told the government to provide health care, but it would be very unlikely that this would evolve into a polite theological discussion about income redistribution—as opposed to, say, a shouting match between a former president and a population that really, really didn't like him.

I see no reason that Alma, who spent most of his time in the judgment seat suppressing a minority religion, should have expected anything different from that religion's followers (and his longtime political enemies) in Ammonihah.

# 29

## Changing Hearts and Minds: Why Alma's Mission Failed while Ammon's Succeeded

LITERATURE MAKES MEANING through structure. One of the most important ways that it does this is by constructing parallel narratives and inviting us to read them together. Anyone who has stayed awake all the way through Hamlet knows that Hamlet and Fortinbras are parallel stories—young princes who must find ways to avenge their fathers without sacrificing their states. Much of what Hamlet means lies in the comparisons and contrasts between these two parallel narratives.

Historians do it too. Literary structure is what turns raw data into history. Take, for example, Bruce Catton's famous framing of the Civil War through the parallel experiences of Grant and Lee. Or, more recently, Ron Chernow's discussion of the Federalist period through the contrasting figures of Hamilton and Jefferson. The literary structure of Chernow's biography was so compelling that, I hear, someone turned it into a pretty good play.

And parallel narratives are all over the Book of Mormon: the anti-Christ stories of Sherem, Nehor, and Korihor; the "prophet-from-nowhere" stories of Abindadi and Samuel the Lamanite.

Mormon, especially, structured his historical record by setting parallel stories next to each other and asking readers to consider both the similarities and the differences. [1]

It is in this context that I would like to discuss two of the most well-known missionary journeys in the Latter-day Saint canon, both of which come from the Book of Alma: Alma's journey to the dissident Nephites in the city of Ammonihah (Alma 8–16), and Ammon's mission to the Lamanites in the Land of Ishmael (Alma 17–20). Initially, the two stories seem like a case study in similarities. Both are undertaken by young men of the same age, with the same basic history, at the same time—and both take up about the same amount of space in the narrative. Beyond that, though, we have mainly contrasts, which, for efficiency's sake, I represent in the following table.

See Table:  **Alma & Ammon**

And all of this brings me to the question in my title: why did Alma's mission fail miserably while Ammon's succeeded beyond anybody's wildest dreams? And yes, I know that a lot of people will object to my calling Alma (a Prophet of God and all) an abject failure. But let's get real. There is no worse outcome for a missionary than seeing the entire city he was sent to save wiped off the face of the earth for their wickedness. I mean, my mission was not hugely successful by any measure, but at least it didn't end with God destroying Fresno. The text invites and even requires us to try to answer the question, "what did Alma and Ammon do differently that lead to such markedly different outcomes in their missionary journeys"?

And I think that the text gives us a compelling answer, which I tried to illustrate in the way that I framed the question in the table below: Alma, unlike Ammon, chose to use pedagogical tools that were completely misaligned with his rhetorical objectives.

Let's not forget that Alma was starting with a lot of baggage. As the Chief Judge of Zarahemla, he had been responsible for the execution of Nehor, the founder of Ammonihah's major religion. He was also at least partly responsible for the civil war between Christians and Nehorites that followed. Therefore, he walked into Ammonihah with all of the credibility of Abraham Lincoln walking into Alabama in 1865—or Lilburn Boggs walking into Salt Lake City in 1850. In a situation like this, there is no way to separate the message from the messenger.

Seemingly oblivious to his rhetorical position, though, Alma begins his mission by calling everybody to repentance, and he follows up by preaching sophisticated sermons and then disputing with people in a series of open forums. Shaming, lecturing, and arguing—these are all common strategies that people use when trying to change other people's minds, even though they rarely ever do that (just peruse the comments section of any controversial blog post and you will see what I mean). These strategies pretty much never bring about the "mighty change of heart" that Alma needed to produce in Ammonihah.

Ammon, on the other hand, employed tools that had nothing to do with trying to change anybody's mind about theological issues. Rather, he concentrated on changing their minds about

| Alma in Ammonihah | Ammon in Ishmael |
|---|---|
| Alma begins his journey to Ammonihah from a position of extreme power and privilege. He is the head of the established church and, for eight years, was also the Chief Judge in the land. And when he resigned that office, he hand picked his successor. Everybody that he encounters knows who he is and knows that he is backed by the power of the state. However, in Ammonihah this works against him, as most of the people in the city were followers of Nehor (whom Alma executed) and supporters of Amlici (against whom Alma fought a bloody civil war). | Ammon enters the land of Ishmael as a stranger with no political or ecclesiastical authority—essentially a blank slate. He is initially taken to the king, who had the power to have him killed or imprisoned on sight, but who, instead, offers him his daughter's hand in marriage. |
| Alma is preaching to Nephites who follow the religion of Nehor. All of them know about the Christian religion, which is the established Church in their land, but they have actively rejected it—often (according to examples found in the text) with the full knowledge that they have placed themselves in opposition to God. | Ammon is preaching to Lamanites who do not appear to have ever encountered Christianity before. They have no knowledge of God or Christ, but they do have an intuitive theology, passed down through generations, of a "Great Spirit" that Ammon is able to build upon to teach them the Christian message. |

Table: Alma & Ammon

| Alma in Ammonihah | Ammon in Ishmael |
| --- | --- |
| Alma is trying to change the behavior of people who know, but do not have actively rejected the truth. He is trying to effect a "mighty change of heart" of the type that he and the Sons of Mosiah experienced during the days that they persecuted the Church. | Ammon is trying to teach people something that they do not know, and the text gives us reasonable assurances that anybody who will honestly consider the claims that Ammon is making will experience a divine confirmation of their truth. |
| Ammon calls the people to repentance, preaches impressive sermons, and contends with the lawyers in the public square. | Ammon volunteers to watch the king's flocks. Then he fights off some bandits. And then he cleans the stables. |
| Alma is unable to persuade the main body of the Ammonihahans to abandon their heresies and their wicked ways, and, as a result, the whole city is destroyed by the Lamanites (but really by God.) | Ammon makes thousands of converts, including King Lamoni (which always helps) and, eventually, the King's father, who is an even bigger king. The entire political landscape of the region is reshaped by the mass conversions of the Lamanites, who resettle in Nephite territories. |

Nephites. He showed them that he was a good servant—that he could be trusted with difficult problems and that he genuinely cared about the king's interests. This, it turns out, is about the best way to go about changing someone's heart. And once a heart changes mightily, intellectual conversion is simply a matter of explaining new facts. It is (as most missionaries learn very quickly) the only way that the discussions actually work.

We can be fairly sure what would have happened if Ammon had gone into the Land of Ishmael with Alma's bag of tools— calling the Lamanites to repentance, delivering long speeches, and arguing with them in the marketplace: the shortest chapter in the entire Book of Mormon would have ended with the words, "and it came to pass that King Lamoni did squish Ammon like unto a bug." Only God, however, knows what might have happened if Alma had gone into Ammonihah, preached fewer sermons, and cleaned more stables.

This is definitely worth pondering when we are trying to persuade other people to change their hearts and their minds.

### Endnotes

1.  See Grant Hardy's *Understanding the Book of Mormon* pp. 152–179 for a discussion of Mormon's frequent use of parallel narratives, including pp. 170–174 specifically on the journeys of Alma and those of the Sons of Mosiah.

# 30

## What Were the "Anti-Nephi-Lehies" Against and Why Does It Matter Today?

A FAIR AMOUNT OF INGENIOUS CRITICISM has gone into explaining why the Lamanites who converted to Christianity and joined the Nephites called themselves by the strange name, "Anti-Nephi-Lehies"—which means something like, "Lehites who were against the Nephites." It doesn't seem to make any sense.

Fortunately, Mormonism has been blessed with a lot of smart people who know a lot of ancient languages. Hugh Nibley, for example, identified an early Indo-European/Semitic usage of "anti–" to mean "facing," making the Anti-Nephi-Lehies "those who face the Nephites." My friend and fellow BCC blogger Kevin Barney identified six possible theories in an excellent 2012 post before offering his own opinion that "anti" could come from the Hebrew *anshae*, which means "people of." [1]

I am not a student of any old languages, so I am unable to assess these constructions. I am, however, a very bad English speller, so I do have some authority when it comes to screwing up my own language. From this perspective, the explanation that makes the most sense to me is that Joseph Smith never meant to

call them "anti–" anything at all. Rather, probably using the very
common (in the 1830s) word "antediluvian" "(before the flood")
as an analog, he labeled the pacifist Lamanite converts "ante-
Nephi-Lehies," or the people of the family of Lehi BEFORE
Nephi (a reading that can be derived from Kevin's #3 option in
the 2012 post).

This, it turns out, can be reasonably well supported by the
earliest textual variants of the Book of Mormon. If we look at
the partially extant Original Manuscript that several scribes
worked on, and at the complete Printer's Manuscript that
Oliver Cowdery created, we see that the Lamanite converts are
called Ante-Nephi Lehites nearly as often as Anti-Nephi Lehites.
Of the twelve uses of the term (or its variants) in the Book of
Mormon, six of them were spelled "Ante" in at least one of the
two original manuscripts before being standardized by the
professional typesetter in E.B. Grandin's office:

Table: **AntiNephiLehies**

| Verse | Original Manuscript | Printer's Manuscript |
|-------|---------------------|----------------------|
| Alma 23:17 | AntiNephiLehies | AntiNephiLehies |
| Alma 24:1 | ANTIN)ephiLehi | AntiNephi Lehi |
| Alma 24:2 | AntiNe(pHILEHI | AntiNephiLehi |
| Alma 24:3 | ANTINEPHILEHI | AntiNephiLehi |
| Alma 24:5 | AnteNephiLehi | AntiNephiLehi |

Table: **AntiNephiLehies**

| Verse | Original Manuscript | Printer's Manuscript |
|-------|---------------------|----------------------|
| Alma 24:20 | AnteNephiLehi | AntiNephiLehi |
| Alma 25:1 | AnteNephiLe(hi) | AnteNephiLehi |
| Alma 25:13 | ANTINEph)iLehi | AnteNephilehi |
| Alma 27:2 | Anti(NEPHILEHI) | Ante-Nephi/-\Lehi |
| Alma 27:21 | AntiNephiLe(hi | AntiNephiLehi |
| Alma 27:25 | ANTINEPHILe)hi | AntiNephiLehi |
| Alma 43:11 | AnteNephi Lehi | AntiNephiLehi |

What this suggests is that Joseph Smith, Oliver Cowdery, and the other scribes were confused about how to spell the phrase that Joseph was speaking, which would be more likely with "ante–" than "anti–," as spelling errors more commonly spell a less familiar word like a more familiar word than the other way around, and far more English constructions begin with "anti–" than with "ante–." [2] The typesetter, John Gilbert, would have standardized the spelling to the version most common in the Printer's Manuscript without really thinking through the finer theological points of the narrative.

But what if he standardized the wrong way? Or what if he was working under the assumption that "anti–" could mean either "against" or "before." It actually can, you know. There are English words that do use "anti–" to mean "before," such as "antiquity," "anticipate," and the Italian-derived "antipasto," which means "what you eat before the meal," or "appetizer." In 1830, spelling was far less standard than it is today, and "anti–" and "ante–" were used interchangeably in words like "antediluvian".

All of this evidence, I would suggest, points to at least a reasonable possibility that the "Anti-Nephi-Lehies" should have been called the "Ante-Nephi-Lehies,", or something like, "the People of Lehi before Nephi." But what in the world does this mean, and why would anyone want to use it to describe themselves?

To understand what it might mean, consider the contemporary usage of "Abrahamic Religion." This has become a shorthand way to describe Judaism, Christianity, and Islam—the three major world religions that claim descent through the line of Abraham. Using this term is also a way to try to erase the divisions that resulted in these three religions becoming such fierce opponents—to suggest that, at our very core, Jews, Christians, and Muslims are all part of a greater family and that we should treat each other accordingly.

I imagine that this is close to what the converted Lamanites meant when they called themselves "Anti-Nephi-Lehies": the term asserts an essential unity in the family of Lehi and erases the great division, which occurred during Nephi's time, that split the family into two groups. The term itself, I believe, attempts to heal the essential, tragic division of the Book of Mormon and the heritage of violence that it produced.

This explains the most significant thing that the Anti-Nephi-Lehies do when they convert to Christianity: they bury their weapons deep within the earth and vow never to engage in violence again. And they then announce that they want their unused weapons to become "a testimony to our God . . . that we have not stained our swords in the blood of our brethren" (Alma 24:15). And succeeding events make clear that they consider both the Nephites (with whom they join) and the Lamanites (to whom they submit to be massacred before picking up their weapons) to be their "brethren."

Of all of the conversion stories in the Book of Alma, I find the conversion of the Anti-Nephi-Lehies to be the most compelling. In the course of converting to Christianity, these Lamanites become genuinely convinced of the essential oneness of God's children. One way that they express this belief is by taking a name that erases the most important division in their culture. Another way that they express it is by refusing to kill anybody ever again, whatever their tribal affiliation may be.

Perhaps more than any of the other Book of Mormon characters who claim to believe in Christianity, then, the Anti-Nephi-Lehies best understand, and are most willing to accept, the burdens of Christian discipleship.

## Endnotes

1.  bycommonconsent.com/2012/07/17/anti-nephi-lehies
2.  The variations in scribal spellings also tell us that Joseph Smith probably pronounced the word "antee", which can be transcribed as either "anti" or "ante" instead of "an-tie", which can only be rendered "anti".

# 31

## Rameumptom

PRETTY MUCH EVERY HUMAN SOCIETY that has ever worshiped a god has seen themselves as that god's chosen people. Such beliefs are rooted in the development of our notions of divinity. Monotheism came fairly late in human history. Most early cultures were either polytheistic, like the Greeks and Romans, who believed in and worshiped multiple deities; or henotheistic, like the early Israelites, who believed that every people had their own god charged with meeting their needs and fighting their battles.

As Hebrew henotheism evolved into modern monotheism, a tribal god came to be seen as the only God in the universe, but He didn't lose all of the characteristics of a tribal deity. Specifically, He still encouraged tribalism—or at least His followers still used Him to further the interests of their tribe. Monotheism was a difficult conceptual shift for the ancient people who made it, and they never really accepted its most important consequence: that God loves all of his children the same. Most people who believe in God still have a hard time accepting that this is true.

I have long believed that the single narrative that unites our Standard Works is the theme of a "chosen people" believing that their relationship to God makes them better than other people and learning—usually the hard way—that they are not. This theme cuts across time periods and continents. It includes the recalcitrant Israelites of the Old Testament, the Pharisees and Sadducees of the New Testament, the prideful Nephites of the Book of Mormon, and the early Latter-day Saints—who imagined that God was going to make their bank solvent and hand them Missouri just because they were his favorite kids. Chosen People Syndrome (CPS) is the common curse of the scriptures.

In Alma 31, Alma and his two younger sons head to Antionum, the land of the Zoramites and the epicenter of the Chosen People Syndrome in the New World. The Zoramites have the most pronounced class differences of any people we encounter in the Book of Mormon. Only the wealthy are permitted to worship in the synagogue, where they climb a high tower called "Rameumptom," or "the Holy Stand" (:21) and pray like this:

> [16] *Holy God, we believe that thou hast separated us from our brethren; and we do not believe in the tradition of our brethren, which was handed down to them by the childishness of their fathers; but we believe that thou hast elected us to be thy holy children; and also thou hast made it known unto us that there shall be no Christ.* [17] *But thou art the same yesterday, today, and forever; and thou hast elected us that we shall be saved, whilst all around us are elected to be cast by thy wrath down to hell; for the which holiness, O God, we thank thee; and we*

*also thank thee that thou hast elected us, that we may not be*
*led away after the foolish traditions of our brethren, which doth*
*bind them down to a belief of Christ, which doth lead their*
*hearts to wander far from thee, our God.* [18] *And again we thank*
*thee, O God, that we are a chosen and a holy people. Amen.*

This prayer makes the Zoramites' belief system pretty clear: they
believe that they are God's favorite people, that he loves them more
than the Nephites (and way more than the Lamanites), that they are
predestined to salvation, and that they are entitled to the wealth
that they possess at the expense of the poor. They are, in other
words, firm believers in "Zoramite exceptionalism," which
convinces them they never need to think highly (or much at all) of
anybody but themselves.

As readers we are shocked by the plainness and directness of the
Zoramite prayer, but we should not be shocked by the overall
message, which pervades the Book of Mormon—and all of the other
Standard Works—from beginning to end. The Zoramites say
directly what the Nephites, Pharisees, and other CPS sufferers say
slightly less directly.

And we say it too. We usually try to avoid the uncouth
directness of the Zoramites. We have masks and code words that
allow us to tell ourselves we are not THAT bad. But all of us are at
least somewhat afflicted with the human belief that God likes us
best. Sometimes, of course, we use other words for "God", like
"reason," "science," "hard work," "fortune," or "natural ability." But
the basic message is the same: we are better than other people, we

deserve to have more stuff than other people, and it is only right that we protect our stuff from our inferiors.

The Book of Mormon, like the Bible and all of the other Standard Works, exists to convince us that we are wrong.

# 32

## King David, Corianton, and Sex

THE LATTER-DAY SAINT SCRIPTURAL TRADITION contains
two great cautionary tales about sex: the first is the story of King
David, who saw Bathsheba bathing on the roof and summoned
her to his quarters—an assignation that ended with the betrayal
and murder of Bathsheba's husband. The second is the story of
Corianton, the son of Alma the Younger, who abandoned his
missionary duties among the Zoramites and dallied with "the
harlot Isabel"—thus imperiling the entire mission and bringing
disrepute on the followers of Christ.

On the surface, these cautionary tales seem to have the
same message, which is something like, "don't follow your sexual
impulses (except under carefully controlled circumstances) or
bad stuff will happen." It's a message that Mormons hear a lot.
But when we start looking at the differences between the two
stories, we start to see very different understandings of human
sexuality and religion at work. And, in this case, the differences
are much more important than the similarities.

Let's start with David, a man who has wives and concubines
all over the place (2 Samuel 5:13). As the king in a polygamous

society, David has very few restraints on his sexual behavior. "Stay away from the wives of top officers who might lead a rebellion against you." That's about it. His actions with Bathsheba show us a man whose appetites and sense of entitlement are so great that he can't even observe the minimal sexual boundaries that his society has set for him. And, of course, things end very badly for him as a result.

But here's the thing: we repeatedly read in the Bible that, whatever else might have strayed, David's heart was always with the Lord. He replaces Saul because he is "a man after [God's] own heart." After he dies, the narrative tells us that his heart was "perfect with the Lord" (1 Kings 11:4) and that he followed the Lord "with all his heart" (1 Kings 14:8). This constant emphasis on David's heart tells us that, as the text presents it, David's sexual impropriety was not tied to any theological error (he continued to believe correctly) or any deficiency of love (he continued to love the Lord with all his heart). This is why, for all of his sins, many people still see David as a hero today.

But what about Corianton's heart? In his lengthy blessing of his son, Alma makes it very clear that Corianton's heart is not right. His sexual sin has resulted in the alienation of his heart from God:

> Suffer not yourself to be led away by any vain or foolish thing; suffer not the devil to lead away your heart again after those wicked harlots. Behold, O my son, how great iniquity ye brought upon the Zoramites; for when they saw your conduct they would not believe in my words. And now the Spirit of the

*Lord doth say unto me: Command thy children to do good, lest
they lead away the hearts of many people to destruction (Alma
39:11–12).*

Corianton's sin, unlike David's, becomes evidence of a deficient
heart. Perhaps even more importantly, though, it also becomes
evidence of a lack of religious understanding. After rebuking
Corianton for his sexual sins for one chapter, Alma spends the
next three chapters correcting his son's theological errors. In
chapters 40–42, Alma takes the unusual step (for someone giving
a blessing) of clarifying doctrines that Corianton has presumably
not understood: the nature of the resurrection, the doctrine of the
spirit world, outer darkness, the corporeality of the afterlife, the
nature of spiritual death, mercy, justice, atonement, and so on.

The curious juxtaposition of moral rebuke and theological
correction in Corianton's blessing casts sexual sin as an essentially
theological problem—either the result or a symptom of a faulty
understanding of the Gospel. This means that the solution
to sexual sin must be theological instruction of the kind that
constitutes the bulk of the blessing. Such an approach implicitly
denies sexuality as a primary part of human identity. We are
not (like King David) sexual beings who have a theology; we are
theological beings who have sex—and whose sexuality must be
entirely contained within theological bounds unless we don't love
God.

There are limits to these kinds of generalizations, of course—
the most obvious being that they work much better for men
than for women. The two texts treat David and Corianton very

differently, but their treatment of Bathsheba and Isabel is almost identical: both women are presented as stumbling blocks to male spiritual progress and not as actual people whose spirituality or sexuality matters for its own sake. This is a huge problem in both texts, and Latter-day Saints all too often pass this flawed understanding on to our daughters by telling them they are responsible—through their dress, their words, and their actions—for making sure that men don't become Davids or Coriantons.

This is one of the reasons that our traditional scriptural cautionary tales have limited instructional value for teaching our youth today. Another is that the two stories end up teaching opposite lessons about what it means to love God, accept the Gospel, and have a sexual identity. Proof-texting both passages to come up with "sex is bad and ugly until you are married, when it becomes a Godly act of co-creation" has not actually worked very well. Mainly it has helped to created several generations of neurotic Mormons. Instead, I would suggest, we should try reading both stories carefully and really grappling with the complicated and difficult issues that they raise for us all.

# 33

## Captain Moroni and Religious Freedom

IT IS NO SECRET that Mormon has a massive man-crush on
Captain Moroni. We see this both in the name of his son and
in his effusive statement that, if everyone were like the good
Captain, "the very powers of hell would have been shaken forever;
yea, the devil would never have power over the hearts of the
children of men" (Alma 48:17). Hero-worship can be a dangerous
trait in a historian, though, and Mormon's unqualified adoration
often conflicts with the story he is trying to tell. A close reading
of one of these conflicts might help us better understand one of
our own.

### Captain Moroni's Freedom Problem

Let's focus here on what I find to be one of the most
problematic passages in the entire Book of Mormon: the
beginning of the war with the Amalickiahites, when Moroni
raises the "Title of Liberty." Here, for the second time in the
Book of Alma, a strong movement arises to overthrow the Reign
of the Judges and restore a monarchy. Because he flatters people
and cares only for power, Amalickiah manages to convince a

lot of people "to destroy the church of God, and to destroy the foundations of liberty which God had granted them" (46:10).

Moroni, of course, will have none of it, and he springs into action. He rends his coat and writes words of freedom on it and rallies all of the Christians (who, as we have already seen, form a majority) to his side. He leads the majority Christians against the Amalickiahites, chases them from the land, cuts off their retreat, and gives them a stark ultimatum:

> *And it came to pass that whomsoever of the Amalickiahites that would not enter into a covenant to support the cause of freedom, that they might maintain a free government, he caused to be put to death; and there were but few who denied the covenant of freedom. (46: 35)*

From what I can tell, we are actually supposed to read that last bit—"and there were but few who denied the covenant of freedom"—with a straight face. Mormon does not appear to recognize the profound irony of forcing people, at the pain of death, to make a covenant to give up their political beliefs and support "the cause of freedom."

As readers, however, we cannot fail to recognize this irony—and to consider its implications for the text. It is the same irony that was identified early in the 20th century by the American rhetorician Kenneth Burke as "the paradox of substance," which he describes in this passage from A Grammar of Motives:

> *This is . . . our paradox of substance. In specifically conceptual*
> *terms, the featuring of a single motive will quickly require one*
> *to grant that its simplicity operates but "in principle." Where it*
> *is treated simply as an "ideal" the paradox enters at the point*
> *where the ideal turns back upon itself. Thus, were we to feature*
> *"freedom" . . . we should eventually have to ask ourselves, as*
> *with Mill, weather it would be in the conformity of this ideal to*
> *"force freedom" upon those who resist it. (105–06)*

Burke is not talking about human motivations here. He is talking
about the way that we tell stories about human motivations.
People don't do anything for only one reason. We are motivated
by a bizarre mix of altruism, self-interest, desire, duty, ambition,
and fear. But when we tell stories about motives, we tend to
discuss them in isolation—to pretend that people do things for
a single, easy-to-understand reason. And this narrative strategy,
Burke insists, will always lead to absurdity when the single motive
is forced back upon itself.

This, in effect, is what happens when Moroni, who is
motivated solely by freedom, forces people who are motivated by
the desire to destroy freedom to swear to support freedom or else
die by the sword.

### Another Point of View

If we assume that the Book of Mormon is what it claims to
be, and that Captain Moroni and Amalickiah were real people,
then we really have to push back against Mormon's simplistic
account of their motives. As Mormon presents it, the contrast

could not be clearer: Moroni wants only to preserve freedom and Amalickiah has no other objective than to destroy it. But human beings don't work that way. Here is how the story might look from the perspective of Amalickiah's supporters. This perspective is just as limited and just as one-dimensional as the one in the text, but it oversimplifies in a different direction—which may help us get closer to the messy and complicated truth:

With this coalition behind him, Amalickiah agitates to change the system of government to something more sensitive to the beliefs of non-Christians. He initially gains some traction with the people, but then the military steps in to defend the government and the Church. Captain Moroni rallies the people around the flag, and both Church and State tell Christians that they cannot support Amalickiah without rejecting God. Moroni solidifies the Christian majority behind him and goes on the offensive. In the name of "freedom," he executes anyone who will not swear allegiance to the political-religious status quo. Amazingly (not!) almost all of the Amalickiahites take the oath.

As I acknowledged earlier, this version of events is just as hostile to Captain Moroni as Mormon's narrative is to Amalickiah. Both narratives reduce their opposition to a single set of clear and easy-to-understand motives—which is a pretty clear indication that neither one gets to what actually happened with the messy and inconsistent human beings involved in the story.

And, perhaps most importantly of all, the two narratives are built around two very different definitions of "freedom." And they are two definitions that remain with us today.

# 34

## How Did Mormon Know That? History and Propaganda in the Amalackiahite War

LET'S START WITH ONE of the most devastating satirical moments in *Don Quixote*. This scene begins in Chapter VIII of the first book. Quixote has already had his adventures with the windmills and the prostitute at the roadside inn, and now he encounters a group of travelers accompanying a lady on her way to meet her husband. Assuming (as he is wont to do) that the woman is being held against her will, Quixote rushes to her defense, starting a fight with a Biscayan gentleman attending her.

Quixote and the Biscayan fight for a while, and the latter gains the advantage. He raises his sword for a killing blow, and just as he does, the narrative stops abruptly—and the narrator tells us that the record doesn't go any further and that this is everything we now can say about Don Quixote de la Mancha. But the narrator refuses to give up. One day he finds an Arabic manuscript in a marketplace that references Dulcinea del Toboso. This turns out to be the work of the famous Arab historian, Cid Hamete Benengeli and, conveniently, it begins at exactly the same point in the story that the previous manuscript left off. The narrative problem is solved.

Cervantes is satirizing works that make historical claims and yet include details that could not have come through the historical record: secret conversations between minor characters, deep motivations of mysterious antagonists, things a character said to his horse—that sort of thing. Cervantes' world was full of historical romances that made these sorts of narrative claims and then violated their own terms by including information that would not have been available to the narrator, yet implied by the text. It was kind of like cheating.

To his credit, Mormon rarely engages in the sort of narrative legerdemain that Cervantes satirizes. He almost never ascribes unknowable motives to characters who are not themselves narrators, nor does he include conversations between characters outside of the hearing of somebody who could have plausibly written them down. This is consistent with the larger claim of the Book of Mormon that Mormon is a historian abridging records from an earlier time into a single narrative.

But Mormon is not perfect, and there are a few exceptions to his general excellence in this regard—perhaps the most glaring of which occur in his description of Amalickiah in the land of the Lamanites. After failing to become King of the Nephites, Amalickiah flees to the land of the Lamanites, where he uses treachery to rise through the ranks and become king. After being given command of forces loyal to the Lamanite king, Amalickiah pretends to join his forces with those of the rebellious commander Lehonti. But he uses a slow poison to kill Lehonti and deliver all of the troops to the King (:18–19)—whom he then murders by having a servant stab him in the heart. He then marries the Queen and becomes King of the Lamanites.

All of this shows us just how evil Amalickiah was, and it proves that the Nephites who supported his earlier bid for the kingship were either evil themselves or sadly deluded. And it demonstrates once and for all that Captain Moroni was right to raise the Title of Liberty, attack the followers of Amalickiah, and force them to recant their beliefs or die. Mormon's description of Amalickiah's treachery clearly justifies all of the questionable things that were done during the early stages of the war.

Or does it?

Alma 47 raises exactly the kind of narrative problem that Cervantes satirized in *Don Quixote*. All of the action occurs well outside of the view of anybody who could plausibly have been a Nephite record keeper. And it describes events that would not have been generally known by either Nephites or Lamanites. Only a very small number of Amalickiah's closest advisers could have known about them, and his hold on power would have depended on absolute secrecy. If any of these advisers were not completely trustworthy, we can be fairly sure that they would not have lasted long in Amalickiah's employ.

So how did Mormon know what happened? Or, to put the question a different way, how do we reconcile the details of the story of Amalickiah with the claims of the narrative itself about what it is and how it knows stuff? At the very least, we have here an uncharacteristic lapse in Mormon's normally conscientious accounting for the origin of the stories that he tells.

There are several ways to answer this question. God could have revealed the information to Mormon, of course. But if God went around revealing things like that we have to wonder why anybody needed to keep records in the first place. A Lamanite prisoner could have spilled the beans. But this strikes me as unlikely, since it was the Lamanites who had to be kept in the dark about Amalickiah for his plans to succeed. This was a secret that the king was keeping from his own people; it had little value to the Nephites as military intelligence.

But it was a story that had tremendous value to the Nephites as propaganda. It would have bolstered the Nephite's claims about the rightness of their cause and the treachery of their opponent. It made Captain Moroni look heroic, and it immediately delegitimized any internal opposition based on residual support for Amalickiah. And if this story could be passed along to the Lamanites, it would undermine their support for their king and make them easier to defeat. It would be hard to imagine a better piece of war propaganda than this.

But the thing about propaganda is that it doesn't have to be true; it just has to be repeated a lot. These sorts of speculation about Amalickiah's rise to power are precisely kinds of rumors that people on one side of a conflict invent about people on the other side. They sound probable enough, account for problematic facts, and completely support the official story of the side doing the propagandizing. And when a war is over, the winning side's propaganda almost always becomes part of the official record. Five hundred years later, a redactor like Mormon would have had a very hard time distinguishing between that official record and the actual facts of history.

# 35

## Can We Judge Captain Moroni by Contemporary Moral Standards?

WELL, OF COURSE WE CAN. We are free to apply any standards we choose to any text that we read. That's how judging stuff works.

But should we judge Book of Mormon characters by contemporary standards on things like religious freedom, separation of church and state, the treatment of prisoners of war, and, well, genocide? After all, this was a different culture and a different time. Should we judge them by the same standards we would apply to someone today?

Again, the answer is, "of course we should"—if we want to take the Book of Mormon seriously on its own terms.

The moral judgments we apply to a narrative depend a lot on what we want to accomplish with the evaluation. Sometimes, all we are trying to do is understand how a culture worked. Thus, as horrified as I am by much of what Achilles does in the *Iliad*, when I teach Homer, I ask students to start with the premise that Achilles represented the ideas of a certain culture and to hold their moral judgments in abeyance and ask, "what does the fact

that the Ancient Greeks considered Achilles a hero tell us about
the Ancient Greeks?"

But this is not quite how the Book of Mormon asks us to read
it. The text goes to great lengths to warn us NOT to read it as a
history of a specific culture, but to see it as a document prepared
specifically for latter-day readers as a source of spiritual wisdom
(see, for example, 1 Nephi 9:2–6). When he completed the text,
Mormon was one of the only two people in the world (the other
being his son) who could even read it. Unlike every other work
in the LDS canon, the Book of Mormon in its final form had no
contemporary audience or rhetorical purpose. We are not merely
part of its extended audience; we are part of its only audience.

And I believe that it has a lot of very important things to
teach us. It says profound things about faith and repentance,
about the urgency of conversion, and about the responsibilities
that we have to each other as members of the Church, just to
name a few. When we apply these things in our lives, we become
better Saints and better people. This is why I see the Book of
Mormon as a central pillar of my faith.

This is also why I insist on judging Book of Mormon
characters by modern moral standards—as they are the only
standards that can be considered part of its rhetorical structure.
Sometimes, the result of such judgment is that I re-evaluate
contemporary moral standards. Sometimes, though, it means that
I re-evaluate the narrative. Like many other texts (Abraham and
Isaac, David and Bathsheba, Thomas Marsh and milk) we need
to decide whether we are going to read the stories of the Book of

Mormon as moral examples or as cautionary tales. Both types of readings can be instructive.

The more I read the latter half of Alma, the more convinced I am that we should read the story of Captain Moroni as a cautionary tale—even though Mormon clearly intended it to be a moral example—as so much of what he does cannot be reconciled with contemporary values that I am not willing to part with. For example:

- He compels people to give up their political beliefs or be executed. (Alma 46:35)
- He arguably engages in ethnic cleansing by driving all of the Lamanites out of the East Wilderness. (Alma 50:9)
- With no clear understanding of the domestic situation, he accuses the elected leader of treason and threatens to lead his army against the government. (Alma 60)
- He negotiates a prisoner exchange in bad faith and then uses a stratagem to break his word. (Alma 54: 3, 20; 55: 2)

Is Captain Moroni's behavior in these instances consistent with the rules of ancient warfare? Absolutely. From the standpoint of any ancient culture, Moroni is a generous, enlightened, and humane military leader. He is a teddy bear compared to any Greek or Roman commander, and, as far as scriptures go, his way of dealing with the Lamanites and the Amalickiahites is far superior to, say, Joshua, who launched a patently genocidal campaign against the Canaanites. But there is no spiritual value for us in evaluating Captain Moroni by the ancient world's rules of war.

To incorporate the lessons of the Book of Mormon in our own lives, we must evaluate it according to our own values. And by contemporary standards, Moroni was not nearly as admirable as Mormon suggests. The narrative of the Amalickiahite war tells of an established state church proclaiming, but not observing, religious freedom and of a commander who frequently suspends the rule of law under the pretense of protecting liberty. When the Governor of Missouri treated Mormons in much the same way that Moroni treated Amalickiahites, we had a thing or two to say about it in the other direction.

Of course everything Captain Moroni did was consistent with the moral understanding of his culture. That's why he was a hero. If our only objective in reading the Book of Mormon is to try to figure out what the Nephites were like, this is all we need to know. This works great for the *Iliad*, but the Book of Mormon should do more. It should teach us how to live in the world today.

We can say that the Book of Mormon was written for us and contains many lessons that can help us in the world today, or we can say that its people were impossibly alien and saw the world through different cultural lenses, so it is unfair to judge them by our standards. But we can't have it both ways at the same time. To the extent that we want to use the Book of Mormon as the basis for anything in our own lives, we have to be willing to evaluate the morality of its characters by the standards of the world that we want to live in.

# 36

## Gadianton, the State, and the Kingdom of God

> Every friend you make, you'll wonder, could just be about
> the money. Every conversation, that's underneath. "Maybe
> he'll give me money." You're not a home teacher. You're not
> even Mahonri Ward anymore. You're three hundred million
> dollars, and that's all you are for the rest of your life.

Eric Samuelsen, *Gadianton*

THERE IS A HEALTHY DEBATE in Mormon Studies—rapidly
approaching a cottage industry—about whether or not the Book
of Mormon's portrayal of the Gadianton Robbers has anything
to do with the anti-Masonic furor that swept across the nation in
the late 1820s. One dead giveaway, say the Masonizers, is that the
term "secret combinations" was commonly (some even say only)
used by the anti-Masonic press in their diatribes against the order
of Freemasons—an order that included such American luminaries
as George Washington, Benjamin Franklin, James Madison, and,
Andrew Jackson.

You will have to Google the rest of the debate, because I have no intention of taking a side. I will say, though, a profound mistrust of secret societies runs deep in human nature. We really don't like it when the people around us are loyal to something that we don't know anything about. And loyalty to something else works directly against cohesion in institutions that are also based on loyalty. Government is one of these institutions; religion is another. Consider this passage from an 1832 issue of the New England Anti-Masonic Almanac:

> *Can you more effectively corrupt the courts of justice, than by tolerating secret oaths of mutual favor and preference between judges, jurors, witnesses and parties? Can you more effectually unstring the arm of the law than by oaths of mutual relief and protection between the sheriff and the culprit? Can you more successfully corrupt your legislative bodies, than by electing representatives who have sworn allegiance to secret combinations? Can you provide more effectual facilities for treason than by enlisting generals and soldiers, who are sworn by oaths of mutual favor to generals and soldiers of the enemy?*

For the anti-Masons of Joseph Smith's day, secret oaths and alliances were a political problem because they threatened to override the political oaths—those taken by public servants, law enforcement officers, witnesses, judges, jurors, soldiers, etc.—that turn a bunch of people into a functioning nation.

We see this pretty clearly with the Gadianton Robbers in the Book of Mormon too. From their inception they try to put people in positions of public trust and then move them through the ranks by assassination. And the oaths that they take to their comrades are always more important than the oaths that they take to the state. This is why Mormon tells us that they would eventually "prove the overthrow, yea, almost the entire destruction of the people of Nephi" (Helaman 2:13). No society can survive long when a near majority of its citizens owe their primary allegiance to something other than the state.

But this isn't really what I think that these passages are about. Or at least it is not the only thing that they are about. The Book of Mormon is a spiritual, rather than a political history, and the story of the Gadianton Robbers contains an important spiritual truth, which is also about loyalty. The truth is this: your God is the thing that you want most, and if this is money, power, or spiritual advancement, you can never have the Kingdom of Heaven. The Kingdom of God is, by definition, the life that is lead in this world by people who want it the most. You cannot, therefore, value the Kingdom less than anything else and still end up with the Kingdom.

Yeah, I know, we can get this straight from the New Testament, where it is the ton-of-bricks message of almost everything that Jesus says. But the New Testament is mainly written to poor people. On the few occasions that Jesus talks to rich people, he mainly tells them to sell everything they have and give it to the poor, which never seems to go over well. Most of what Jesus says about wealth is theoretical; his first generation of followers didn't have very much of it.

But the Nephites at the time of Helaman have wealth in abundance. There is a lot of money around in this world, which has the predictable effect of making it the thing that people want most. The Gadianton Robbers are simply more upfront about this than others. They announce, or at least tell their followers, that money is the most important thing and they will have to sacrifice everything else to get it. As a result, they immediately became one of the largest and most influential institutions in the land.

The Gadianton Robbers of the Book of Mormon are simply the mirror image of the Kingdom of God in the New Testament. They are both avenues through which people get what they want the most. And the terms are exactly the same: you can only have it if it is the thing that you want more than anything else, that you are willing to sacrifice everything else for, and that you direct all of your time and attention to create. But you can't have them both because you cannot devote 100% of yourself to more than one thing. It's just math.

The best guide I know to this aspect of the Book of Mormon is Eric Samuelsen's magnificent 1997 play, *Gadianton*. The play is set in St. George, Utah, and nearly all of the major characters are Latter-day Saints struggling (or at least saying that they are struggling) to live their religion and create Zion on Earth. They also work in a corporate environment seriously contemplating layoffs that will affect the lives of thousands of fellow Saints. And Samuelsen skillfully maneuvers the characters into positions where they have to choose between having money—ranging from obtaining hundreds of millions of dollars to having a minimal level of job security—and acting with compassion and Christ-like love towards others.

The choices that these characters make tell us what they really value the most. And (hopefully) most of us will be profoundly disturbed by several of them—such as the choice of the company president to take a $300 million payout that comes at the cost of 2,000 jobs and the choice of a genuinely moral Bishop to sacrifice his family's livelihood in order to protect one of his parishioners. How many of us could have made the latter choice, and how many of us would have failed to make the former? The answers say a lot about what we want most.

Samuelsen's *Gadianton* gets to the core of the spiritual warning contained in the Gadianton Robbers narrative—which is that we get what we want most (which is not at all the same as getting what we say we want most). The Gadianton Robbers simply formalize the real governing values of a great many people in Helaman's day—and our own. They show us that both great wealth and the Kingdom of God get built exactly the same way: by people who want it more than anything, who are willing to sacrifice everything to it, and whose primary loyalty is to the forces that create it.

# 37

## Nephi's Lament and the Perils of Historiolatry

NEPHI SON OF HELAMAN lived in a world turned upside down. During the course of his lifetime, the Nephites went from being the good guys who had the Church of Christ in their midst to being the bad guys controlled by secret combinations, robbers, wealth-getters, and other doers of dastardly deeds. The Lamanites, on the other hand, had become the righteous ones—the ones who had to warn the Nephites to return to God. So it is certainly understandable that Nephi longed for better days:

> Oh, that I could have had my days in the days when my father Nephi first came out of the land of Jerusalem, that I could have joyed with him in the promised land; then were his people easy to be entreated, firm to keep the commandments of God, and slow to be led to do iniquity; and they were quick to hearken unto the words of the Lord—Yea, if my days could have been in those days, then would my soul have had joy in the righteousness of my brethren. But behold, I am consigned that these are my days, and that my soul shall be filled with sorrow because of this the wickedness of my brethren. (Helaman 7:7–9)

Nephi's Lament is both tragic and poignant, but like most
such tributes to times past it is also historically problematic.
The original Nephi did not spend a lot of time rejoicing in the
righteousness of his brethren, as two of these brethren kept trying
to kill him. His was perhaps the most divided generation in the
Book of Mormon—the time when the people of Nephi split into
the warring factions that persist throughout the text.

But Nephi's lament is understandable. We all like to look
back to a time when things were better. I once had an institute
teacher tell the entire class that the 1950s were the high point
of American righteousness. He was remembering Wally and the
Beaver, praying in school, and movies where nobody swore. He
conveniently forgot the Klan, the lynchings, and the rampant
persecution of anyone who didn't look or act like a member of
the Cleaver family. But I do it too. I will never agree that anybody
making music today can compare to Queen and Styx. My dad felt
the same about Harry Belafonte and Johnny Mathis.

There is something deep in our cognitive architecture that
causes us to idolize past times and deprecate present ones. We
tend to filter out the bad stuff in our memory and remember
everything being better than it really was. Conversely, we tend
to filter out the good things in our current line of sight. I suspect
that this has an evolutionary basis. Keeping track of threats is
much more important to our survival than smelling the roses. It
is only in memory that our Pleistocene forbearers could afford to
take their eyes off the lions, tigers, and bears. Natural selection
does not care whether or not we are happy, and pessimism is a
much more adaptive outlook than hope.

But historiolatry has its discontents. For one thing, it is almost never accurate. Past times were never as good as we imagine them, and the present day rarely sucks as much as our Facebook feeds would suggest. If Nephi were really reading the plates of his namesake, he might have realized that the time he was longing for was an era of bitter conflict and great unrighteousness. And if he were looking around his own society a little bit more, he might see that the mass conversions of Lamanites to the Church of Christ was one of the most significant things to have happened in his world since the original divide.

Furthermore, using an idealized version of the past to denounce the sins of the present traps us into a destructive narrative of perpetual decline. It is a narrative that religious people have always loved, despite its fundamental hopelessness: the world was once almost perfect, and it has been getting steadily worse ever since. The high point of civilization—be it King David, Charlemagne, the time of Lehi, or the Eisenhower Era—has passed, and all we can do is continue our slide into suckitude until God decides to wreck the place and start over. In the meantime, the best we can do is criticize "the world" and thank God that we are the only righteous ones in it.

In this way, generations of human beings have deprived themselves of hope in anything but a cataclysmic end and have let their misplaced nostalgia for a golden age that never was blind them to the beauties of the present world—which is, in every way that matters, a precious gift from God.

# 38

## Samuel the Lamanite and Who We Call a Prophet

We and the prophet have no language in common. To us the moral state of society, for all its stains and spots, seems fair and trim; to the prophet it is dreadful. So many deeds of charity are done, so much decency radiates day and night; yet to the prophet satiety of the conscience is prudery and flight from responsibility. Our standards are modest; our sense of injustice tolerable, timid; our moral indignation impermanent; yet human violence is interminable, unbearable, permanent.... The prophet's ear perceives the silent sigh.

Abraham Heschel, *The Prophets*

I WAS WELL INTO MY THIRTIES before I realized that Latter-day Saints use the word "prophet" in places that most religious people don't. For us, it is a specific office within a well-organized hierarchy. We rightly apply the term to the President of the Church and to the other fourteen members of the First

Presidency and the Quorum of the Twelve. Someone is a
"prophet" by virtue of their standing within an institution.

There are people like this in the scriptures, and the Book
of Mormon is full of them, prophets all: Nephi, Jacob, Mosiah,
Alma, Other Alma, Helaman, and Other Nephi, to name just
a few. These are all, in effect, presidents of stuff. Heads of the
Church (and in some cases the state) and keepers of the plates.
These fellows teach, preach, expound, and exhort with an
authority that the Book of Mormon and modern revelation both
label "prophetic."

But there is another kind of prophecy at play in the Book of
Mormon—one that comes much closer to the more traditional
Jewish and Christian understanding of the term. Abraham
Heschel's 1962 classic *The Prophets* is a good place to get a basic
understanding of this kind of prophecy, which almost never
comes from people with positions of institutional power. Rather,
it comes TO people of institutional power from people on the
margins of society. And it uses a very different kind of language
to speak in the Name of the Lord.

Only two figures in the Book of Mormon fit this model of
prophecy: Abinidai and Samuel the Lamanite, who frame the
more-or-less contiguous narrative that constitutes the bulk of the
Nephite story. Of the two, Samuel is the more prophet-y. In fact,
he is the best example that we have in the Book of Mormon of a
"prophet" as the term is understood by biblical scholars. There are
three areas where I think that this is significant.

## Samuel is an Alien

Foreignness is part of his very name, "Samuel the Lamanite," and it is the first thing we learn about him when he is introduced in the Book of Mormon (Helaman 13:2). This is important because both literal and figural alienation are important to the standard definition of a prophet. Prophets frequently come from somewhere else (and very often they seem to come from nowhere at all), and, as Heschel argues, "the prophet is a lonely man. He alienates the wicked as well as the pious, the cynics as well as the believers, the priests and the princes, the judges and the false prophets."

Prophets are cast out, as Samuel is cast out when he begins to preach, because they alienate everybody and nobody wants them around. The standard works give us no better symbol for the marginality and irreducible otherness of prophetic discourse than Samuel the Laminate, the despised foreign prophet, standing on the city wall and preaching repentance to those who have cast him out of their midst.

## He Forcefully Criticizes the Social Structure of His Society

The prophets of the Old Testament got angry about many things, but nothing roused their ire (and, if they are to be believed, the Lord's) more than social injustices. Social structures that elevated the rich and abased the poor were (and are) fundamentally opposed to the justice of God, and they make it impossible to build the Kingdom of God, which requires a completely different view of material wealth. Thus, when Samuel says things like this in Helaman 13:21, he is tapping into a very rich vein of prophetic material:

> Behold ye, the people of this great city, and hearken unto my words; yea, hearken unto the words which the Lord saith; for behold, he saith that ye are cursed because of your riches, and also are your riches cursed because ye have set your hearts upon them, and have not hearkened unto the words of him who gave them unto you.

We should also note here that Samuel's entire concern appears to be with the deep structures of society. He does not predict the immediate demise of the people because of their wickedness. The destruction that he sees is 400 years in the future (13: 5, 9), after the coming of Christ and a long period of righteousness. As a prophet, he sees this, but he also sees a cancer embedded deep in the social structure that will result in the destruction of the entire people.

### He Has No Authority Beyond His Vision & His Voice

For me, the strangest thing about Samuel is the role that the official Church plays in the story, which is to say that the official Church plays no role at all. This is not because it is absent from the world. Nephi, the official prophet and custodian of the plates, is extremely active at the time of Samuel, having just been given the sealing power and started (and stopped) a famine in the land. And yet, there appears to be no coordination between Nephi and Samuel. Neither one mentions the other, or suggests that people seek out the other, or hosts the other for a fireside or live Christmas broadcast. As did nearly all of the prophets of the Old Testament, Samuel works directly under the Lord and entirely outside of the existing ecclesiastical structures.

Even in his capacity as record keeper, Nephi fails to take Samuel's prophecies seriously. This, at least, is the judgment of Jesus Christ in 3 Nephi 23: 9–12, when he asks to see the records and wonders why they do not include things that Samuel was clearly instructed to say. Nephi sheepishly admits that these portions of Samuel's prophecy were not written down (it is unclear whether or not Samuel's words were recorded at all). Jesus tells him to fix it.

This omission should not surprise us. As I said at the start, there have always been two different kinds of prophets in the LDS scriptural tradition. Prophets like Alma and Nephi come from the center of their social world. They lead a Church organization and exercise authority as a function of their institutional position. But we have also always had prophets like Samuel, who come from the margins and speak with an urgency inspired by their vision and an authority derived only from the power of their voice.

Those of us who covenant to follow the prophets would do well to glance from time to time at the outskirts of our communities to see what despised and disturbing figures might be standing on a wall and shouting at us with a voice and a vision that come directly from God.

## Endnotes

1.  A third figure, Lehi, is a prophet in this sense in Jerusalem, before the Book of Mormon narrative begins, but he operates a different way in the text itself.

# 39

## Seven Ways of Looking at a Lamanite

FOR MODERN READERS, one of the most awkward and difficult passages in the Book of Mormon occurs in the second chapter of 3 Nephi, amid the resurgence of the Gadianton Robbers and the big to-do over the signs for Christ's birth. It's the passage where the righteous Lamanites have the curse removed from their skin, turning them into a lovely shade of white:

> And it came to pass that those Lamanites who had united with
> the Nephites were numbered among the Nephites; And their
> curse was taken from them, and their skin became white like
> unto the Nephites; And their young men and their daughters
> became exceedingly fair, and they were numbered among
> the Nephites, and were called Nephites. And thus ended the
> thirteenth year. (3 Nephi 2: 14–16)

This passage acts like a corrosive acid on the ways that we try to explain away the Lamanite curse narrative that frames much the Book of Mormon. It reminds us that the Book of Mormon equates dark skin color with unrighteousness, and it mocks our efforts to say that it really isn't about race.

In light of a problematic passage like this, I believe, it is important for us to remember something that I have written about a number of times in this series: that nearly every passage in the Book of Mormon has to be filtered through multiple narrative perspectives before we can make any meaning out of them in the world that we inhabit. This filtering process (if we take the Book of Mormon seriously as what it claims to be) includes multiple sites where information could be colored by social biases and perceptions.

The term "Lamanite" is especially prone to this kind of filtering throughout the Book of Mormon. Any attempt to explain what the term means in a passage set around the time of Christ has to account for at least seven cultural filters, each one of them a potential site for narrative unreliability. Let me elaborate:

### Nephi's Mythic Past

In reading the Book of Mormon, we very often fail to account for the effect that large time spans have on the language and culture of oral societies with limited scribal literacy. Six hundred years pass between Laman and Lemuel and the Nephi of this passage. We live in a highly literate culture, and very few of us know much about what went on in Europe in 1416—the time of the anti-popes and the Wars of the Roses. Even highly specialized scholars with access to vast library resources have to do a lot of guesswork in these areas. And we know next to nothing about the culture of the Americas 50 years before Christopher Columbus was born.

In ancient cultures with limited literacy—precisely what the Book of Mormon presents us with—600-year-old history is always a mix of fact and folklore, tending towards the latter. This is roughly the amount of time that passed between Confucius and the Righteous Kings, or between Plato and the Trojan War, or between Henry VIII and King Arthur. The Lehite family in which the ancestors of the Lamanites and the ancestors of the Nephites were brothers may well have functioned 600 years later as a sort of cultural unity talking point, much as the phrase "Abrahamic Religions" does today. Things this far in the distant past are only remembered to the extent that they matter to the world of the present.

### Nephi's Recent History

For Nephi, the Lamanites were also the main enemies in two recent hemispheric conflicts—much as, say, the Germans function in the recent history of the United States. There would still have been people alive who remembered these conflicts, or whose parents remembered them, causing Lamanites to be viewed with suspicion. But the recent history is more complicated, as a number of Lamanites fought for the Nephites during these wars, especially the most recent one.

And there is substantial textual evidence that the term "Lamanite" was emptied, or nearly emptied of its ethnic significance during the time of the Second War. To the extent that this is true, the assertion that Lamanites had a miraculous change in skin color during the time of Nephi becomes almost impossible to defend literally, since the category "Lamanite" had already ceased to describe a literal physiognomy.

## Nephi's Current Reality

Through internal textual evidence, we can date the passage above rather exactly to the year 13 AD. At this time, the Nephites are facing another major war, but it is not with the Lamanites per se. The Gadianton Robbers—whose ranks include both Nephites and Lamanites—have replaced the Lamanites as the enemy of record. This means that some Nephites and some Lamanites were (in narrative terms) "the good guys," while other Nephites and other Lamanites were "the bad guys." Given that the entire Book of Mormon narrative has been built around spiritual distinctions with physiological manifestations, it makes some sense that this new configuration of alliances would be invested with the same ethnic logic. This would not require any skin-lightening miracles from God, just the exercise of a fertile narrative imagination.

## Mormon's Mythic Past

Let us also remember that 400 more years pass between Nephi and Mormon, who is the final redactor of the story. Once again, 400 years in a primarily oral culture is enough time for history to turn into folklore. (This is about the amount of time that has passed since the Pilgrims landed on Plymouth Rock. Think how that plays out in our current Thanksgiving celebrations). And if we look at the paucity of record-keeping during much of this time—a single chapter of 4th Nephi covers the entire 400 years—we have little reason to doubt that most of what Mormon understood about the previous 400 years came from highly unreliable oral sources rather than labor-intensive chiseling on golden plates.

### Mormon's Current Reality

Mormon also spent most of his life fighting a cataclysmic war against the Lamanites of his day. He was not in a position to reflect on these racial issues philosophically. According to the terms of the narrative, he was writing at a time when the Nephites had been wiped out by the Lamanites. We have no idea what Nephites and Lamanites might have looked like in 400 AD, but Mormon knew, and he had a strong incentive to describe his Lamanites negatively. One way to do this would be to highlight elements of the historical record that emphasized the divine disfavor of the ancestors of his current enemies—including the belief that the righteous ones were all made to look more like him.

### Nineteenth-Century Views on Race

The LDS Church no longer considers the curse of Laman to be an explanation for the skin color of contemporary Native Americans. But this is a fairly recent position. There is no doubt that Joseph Smith and his contemporaries held this story out as an etiological tale to explain something that, in 1830, did not have a good explanation—or at least an explanation that could map onto the larger culture's belief in the inerrancy and totality of the biblical record. Tracing the origin of the Native Americans back to the Lost Ten Tribes was important to the narrative that Joseph was constructing—a narrative that the Church now rejects and that makes absolutely no sense in the world that we now inhabit.

Even if we consider Joseph Smith to be the translator of a legitimate ancient record, we cannot ignore the role that translators play in shaping narratives. Translation is never a simple process of substituting one word for another. It is a creative intellectual endeavor that requires the translator to fill a lot of narrative gaps. This is especially true of translations from ancient languages that nobody has ever heard of and original texts that nobody has ever seen. We must always remember that Joseph Smith was constructing a narrative to explain things in his culture too, using a translation process that we understand almost nothing about.

## Twenty-first Century Views on Race

Finally, we have to acknowledge our own filters and biases. We live in a modern society with a lot of unresolved racial tensions, with a lot of very visible, vigorously contested questions about the meaning of various racial identities. This is true across the culture, but it is especially true of people (like me) who went to graduate school in the humanities during the 1990s. I took multiple classes on racial identity in literature, and we examined passages like this in dozens of works of literature from other cultures in order to tease out those cultures' racial assumptions and biases.

I don't think that this is a bad thing. It makes sense that we study literature for what it can tell us about the things that we consider important. But we also have to acknowledge that, when we do this, we are spending considerably more energy unweaving baskets than the original authors spent weaving them. The fact that these issues are so important to us becomes yet another filter of the original text, causing us to create scholarly interpretations that the original authors would be unlikely to recognize or acknowledge.

So, what does all of this tell us? Not much, but also everything. It does not tell us what Nephites or Lamanites really looked like. Nor does it tell us whether or not righteous Lamanites went through a miraculous whitening process in 13 AD that signified the removal of a curse. And it tells us absolutely nothing about Native Americans today. What I would suggest, however, is that the Book of Mormon contains enough narrative complexity to make us suspicious of the most simple and obvious readings of this passage—readings that rely too much on both magic and a racist God.

# 40

## The Sermon on the Mount and the Sermon at the Temple: A Study in Rhetorical Contrasts

MY SCRIPTURES STILL HAVE GREEN MARKINGS in Matthew and 3 Nephi that highlight all of the differences between the Sermon on the Mount (Matt. 5–7) and the Sermon at the Temple (3 Nephi 12–14). I did this on my mission because I thought it was important. "Blessed are the poor IN SPIRIT WHO COME UNTO ME," says the Book of Mormon, lest we think that actual poverty is either necessary or sufficient. And don't forget that the Book of Mormon doesn't say "Thy Kingdom come" in the Lord's Prayer. That's because it already has. These comparisons got me through my mission, a BYU term paper, and the first two times I taught Gospel Doctrine.

It is only recently that I have begun to see what a gnat-straining, camel-swallowing approach to the texts this is. Read from one perspective, of course, the two texts are extremely similar and we can learn a lot by comparing the small differences. From another perspective, however, the texts don't even have much in common. This other perspective is sometimes called "rhetorical criticism."

Some background: a rhetorical interpretation assumes that meaning is produced by the combination of a text and a rhetorical context—a situation in which somebody is trying to use language to do something involving someone else. Words without rhetorical context are both meaningless and impossible. There is no such thing as no context; words are always trying to do something, teach something, or persuade somebody.

But the exact same words can shift meaning dramatically when they are placed in different contexts. If I call someone "dad," it makes a difference if I am talking to a) my father; b) my boss; or c) an older gentleman who is taking too long in the grocery line. My relationship to the speaker, my immediate rhetorical purpose, and our shared context all act on the exact same words to produce very different meanings. This is the major reason that it makes no sense to read the scriptures as acontextual proof texts that "simply mean what the words say." There is always a context. And it always matters.

The New Testament context for the Sermon on the Mount (and I speak here only of how it is presented in the text, not of a knowable historical situation) goes something like this: Jesus has recently been baptized by John the Baptist and completed a 40-day fast, and now he is ready to start his ministry. He has already chosen his disciples and attracted some attention as both a teacher and a healer, but the Sermon on the Mount is his first big-time gig—a make-it or break-it event that will cement his reputation as a Teacher of the Word. He does not come to the audience with any kind of institutional authority. Whatever authority he ends up with will have to come solely from the power of his words.

Compare this to the Book of Mormon context. Here, people have been talking about him by name, and arguing about his coming, for 600 years. For the last 30 years or so, they have been measuring time by the signs that they saw at his birth. And over the past few months, he has trashed the whole country. Tempests, terrible thunder, the earth divided asunder, Zarahemla burned to the ground, Moroni sunk in the ocean, Moronihah swallowed by a mountain. And then things really start to go downhill. When all of this is over, he descends on the survivors wearing a white robe and glowing in the dark. Nobody has to wonder whether or not he has power. He does not have to persuade anyone to accept his authority.

So here's my point: given the terrible destruction that has just been visited on the people of the Book of Mormon, and the supernatural effects that accompany his visit, he simply cannot speak to the people the same way he did when he was the carpenter's kid from Nazareth. Even if the words on the page are exactly the same, both the relationship of the speaker to the audience and the overall rhetorical context could not be more different. In the Book of Mormon, Jesus doesn't have to display power through his words. Everybody knows that he has power. He is now a God telling his followers what he expects them to do.

So take a verse like 3 Nephi 12:12 (Matthew 5:13):

*Verily, verily, I say unto you, I give unto you to be the salt of the earth; but if the salt shall lose its savor wherewith shall the*

*earth be salted? The salt shall be thenceforth good for nothing,*
*but to be cast out and to be trodden under foot of men.*

In the Sermon on the Mount, this has a very specific referent.
Jesus is talking both to and about the Jews, who see themselves as
the Chosen People—the "salt of the earth." Jesus takes this
formulation and hurls it back in their faces, saying that salt
does not exist for its own sake, but to improve what it comes in
contact with. Jews, in other words, should not consider themselves
superior to other people because of their special relationship
with God. That relationship means that they have a responsibility
to improve their world and benefit others. As John the Baptist
has already pointed out (Matt. 3:9), God can make Children of
Abraham out of rocks.

The Book of Mormon context is very different. For one thing,
there are no "chosen people"—everybody is an Israelite, so the
Abrahamic covenant cannot be used to sort people into different
piles. Furthermore, a good chunk of the population has already
been trodden under the foot, not of man, but of God. When Jesus
speaks these words, he is largely explaining something that has
already happened, in effect telling the people present that they
have passed the test and been judged good salt. And when he
talks about troddening, he is not using a metaphor.

This is just one example, but they are throughout the text.
When we look at the tremendous contextual differences between
Matthew 5–7 and Matthew 12–14, we can't come away with the
idea that Jesus preached the exact same (or even nearly the same)
sermon in the Book of Mormon that he preached to the people

in Galilee. Nothing at all about these two sermons was the same except for the words. And words are only a small part of what we talk about when we talk about meaning.

# 41

## Losing Zion: Economic Inequality and the Tragedy of Fourth Nephi

BOOKS LIKE FOURTH NEPHI remind us that the Book of Mormon does not really present itself as a continuous thousand-year history. It is more like three snapshots of periods within a thousand year history: one from the beginning, one from the middle, and one from the end. And we should always keep in mind that cultures and languages change a lot in a thousand years. There is as much cultural and historical distance between Mormon and Nephi as there is between 21st Century Americans and William the Conqueror.

For me, this makes the very brief transitions between snapshots the most fascinating parts of the entire Book of Mormon. Fourth Nephi, for example, gives us 400 years of history in about four pages. Imagine trying to write a four-page history of the United States from Plymouth Rock to Donald Trump. What would you include? What would you exclude? How would you frame the entire American narrative in 49 verses? That is roughly the task that Mormon had when putting together 4th Nephi.

I find it telling, then, that Mormon frames the narrative as
a spiritual tragedy—something like: "How the Only People in
History to Achieve Zion and Not Get Taken Up into Heaven
Managed to Screw It Up and Make the World a Living Hell in
Only Two Hundred Years." Undoubtedly, this narrative leaves
out a lot. It took the people of Mormon's day 200 years—almost
the entire history of the United States—to go from the Kingdom
of God to "solitary, poor, nasty, brutish, and short." This is a
snail's pace compared to, say, *Lord of the Flies*, where the same
transformation takes about a week. But the stories are about the
same.

The arc of 4th Nephi bisects almost perfectly into a "before"
and "after" picture of the people it describes. The first 23 verses
and 200 years describe a people who have achieved Zion. Verses
24–25 describe a turning point. And the final 23 verses show
how Zion is lost in another 200 years. This is the only passage
that I am aware of in the Standard Works that gives us point-by-
point instructions on how to destroy an ideal society. Mormon
apparently felt that we needed to know about this, and I suspect
he was right.

So, how does it work? How does the Kingdom of God, once
built, slip from our grasp? Well, it starts with tolerating economic
inequality, which, by definition, cannot exist in Zion:

> And now, in this two hundred and first year there began to
> be among them those who were lifted up in pride, such as the
> wearing of costly apparel, and all manner of fine pearls, and of
> the fine things of the world. And from that time forth they did

*have their goods and their substance no more common among*
*them. And they began to be divided into classes; and they began*
*to build up churches unto themselves to get gain, and began to*
*deny the true church of Christ. (24–26)*

The order here matters. The first thing to go was the economic foundation of people holding all things in common. And the first division to enter the Kingdom was a division into economic classes. Immediately thereafter, the social and religious structures of society shift to accommodate the class structure. Those who had stuff began to create religions that justified their stuff. They began to pretend that God wanted them to have all the stuff they could get. And they convinced themselves that He wanted them to have more stuff than other people.

And then something really remarkable (and not in a good way) happens: the people who have been living without any kind of ethnic and national distinctions for the better part of 200 years revive the old ones and start applying them to themselves for totally new reasons:

*And it came to pass that in this year there arose a people who*
*were called the Nephites, and they were true believers in Christ;*
*and among them there were those who were called by the*
*Lamanites—Jacobites, and Josephites, and Zoramites; Therefore*
*the true believers in Christ, and the true worshipers of Christ,*
*(among whom were the three disciples of Jesus who should*
*tarry) were called Nephites, and Jacobites, and Josephites, and*

*Zoramites. And it came to pass that they who rejected the gospel were called Lamanites, and Lemuelites, and Ishmaelites. (36–38)*

From a cultural context, this would be roughly the same as our mixing all of our ethnic divisions together and then dividing up into people called "Normans," "Ring Danes," and "Jutes," depending on our religious affiliation. But there you go.

Zion is a society of one heart and mind, and it is instructive to see how that precarious unity can be destroyed. The first division—and the one that drives all of the others—is economic: the division into rich and poor. And then everything else in society moves to accommodate this division. The people create different religions to justify the existence of rich and poor. And then they create ethnic divisions out of thin air to represent their religious divisions.

More than any other part of our Standard Works, Fourth Nephi shows us what is possible when human beings embrace Zion and work with all their heart, might, mind, and strength to bring about the Kingdom of God. And it also shows us the one essential social division that will prevent the Kingdom from ever happening.

This is all terribly inconvenient, of course, as we would all like our religious truths to be separate from our political reality except when it comes to abortion and same-sex marriage. But Mormon really doesn't leave us much choice. Economic equality is a non-negotiable in Zion, and economic inequality is a deal breaker. So, as much as we don't want it to be true, the question, "What have you done today to decrease economic equality among your fellow human beings?" is completely inseparable from the question, "What have you done today to bring about the Kingdom of God?"

# 42

## Meeting Mormon

ONE THING ABOUT NARRATIVES is that you always have to be revising your assumptions as you get more information. What you think you are reading at the beginning of a book may not be what you will think you have read when you are done. We see this dramatically in "surprise ending" kinds of narratives—think of the ending of movies like *The Sixth Sense* or *The Usual Suspects*, which force you to reinterpret everything you have seen in light of the information presented in the last reel.

All narratives work this way. We see this very clearly in long sagas. Knowing that Harry Potter is a Horcrux, for example, changes the way that we read all of the books in the series. But we see it in shorter texts too. It is one of the ways that narratives tickle our cognitive fancies. They give us pleasure by hiding information from us, revealing it in stages, and then making us stretch back to reinterpret what we thought we knew in the light of what we finally discover.

And yet, for all of this, there has never been a narrator quite like Mormon, the final redactor of all of the Book of Mormon (and the reason it has that name). In one sense, we meet Mormon fairly early on in the narrative. He pops in for a second in "Words of Mormon" and does his first "time passes" gloss of a couple hundred years of history. And we hear his voice throughout Mosiah, Alma, Helaman, 3 Nephi, and the second "time passes" gloss called 4 Nephi. By the time we get to the actual Book of Mormon, its main character is an old friend.

Except that we don't actually know much about him or the context in which he lived until we get to his very own book. We know (from the title page) that the whole Book of Mormon was written by his hand and "sealed up, and hid up unto the Lord" by Moroni. And we know from the Words of Mormon that Moroni is his son and that the two of them have "witnessed almost all the destruction of the . . . Nephites" (Words of Mormon: 2). And we know that he was tasked with abridging the records of the 150 years or so between the time of King Benjamin to the coming of Christ.

Like everybody who writes anything, Mormon was trying to understand something about the world he lived in. No matter how hard we try to do otherwise, we must ultimately write only from our own perspective. That's how perspectives work. Furthermore, all historians must use history to understand something about their own present, and Mormon was no different. Consider:

• Mormon was a military leader and a brilliant strategist. Military life was what he knew best, which may account for the overwhelming emphasis on military actions and military strategy in the Books of Alma and Helaman.

When former generals write history books, they almost always overemphasize military history, and there is no reason to think that Mormon was any different.

- Mormon spent most of his life in a society that was split into two opposing factions, called "Nephites" and "Lamanites." During his time, these were clearly delineated factions involved in a war of extermination. If we read back through Mormon's narrative, we often find him trying to fit the conflicts that he is writing about into a similar "Nephite vs Lamanite" narrative, even when other indications in the text suggest that the dichotomy is not nearly as concrete as it was during Mormon's day.

- The Gadianton Robbers appeared to be very strong during Mormon's day (1:18–19), which would have made it important for him to trace the origins of this secret society back as far into history as he could. His own experience with the Robbers might also have tempted him to extrapolate from it in order to explain the effects that the same group had on historical events.

- Finally, Mormon lived at a time when the Nephites were wicked, weak, and in the process of being exterminated. A natural instinct of those who write at such times is to focus on the glories of the past, perhaps even exaggerating the extent of military victories and the role of important cultural heroes. Many of the stories of the greatness of David and Solomon trace back to the days of Israel's captivity in Babylon, just as many of the exploits of King

Arthur were created when England was being conquered
by the Normans.

What all of this points to is the fact that Mormon was creating a
story whose ending he knew before he even started. The narrative,
therefore, had to be a tragedy, and the story he crafted had to be a
story of decline, because that is how he knew it was going to end.
Like the great English historian Edward Gibbon, who wrote *The
Decline and Fall of the Roman Empire*, Mormon was writing a story
that had to end badly. This doesn't mean that he got the history
wrong, but it does mean that, like Gibbon, Mormon framed the
entire narrative according to what he knew about how it was
going to end. Such a perspective contains both great blindnesses
and great insights. And, as readers, we must be aware of both.

# 43

## We've Seen this Show Before (and We Will See It All Again): Ether and the Patterns of Sacred History

FROM A NARRATIVE PERSPECTIVE, the Book of Ether is a frustrating problem. It comes just as the Book of Mormon is winding down—after the chief redactor hands the whole work over to his son, who then writes several chapters of his own and seems to say goodbye. And then, *wham*, the narrative hits us with 1600 years or so of history that we didn't know about before. At precisely the moment that we anticipate closure, the narrative opens up wider than it has ever been.

I want to try to answer the question, "why"? That's kind of a hard question, because any possible answer will be colored by one's assumptions about what the Book of Mormon is. One answer is, "God wanted it this way." But even if we accept that as unproblematically true, all it does is shift the uncertainty to a new question. Why did God want it this way? What is the spiritual value of this particular story in the place that it occupies?

If we assume that Joseph Smith created the Book of Mormon entirely from his imagination, we have the same problem: why

would any rational narrator—human or divine—choose to end
a lengthy epic story by inserting another, highly compressed
epic story into the closing lines. It would be like Homer having
Odysseuscome home, reunite with his son, and then tell the
entire story of the Trojan War in Book XXIII—right before going
on to kill the suitors. Someone reading the Book of Mormon
for the first time, with no understanding of its structure, would
experience just such a disjuncture.

But something else happens too—something that I found
particularly striking when I read the Book of Mormon this year in
the 1830 edition (i.e, the version without verse division that reads
more like a novel). The story of the Jaredites contains so many
similarities to two other narratives—the narrative of the Nephites
and the Lamanites and the narrative of the Coming forth of the
Book of Mormon—that it turns isolated incidents into repeating
patterns. It does this through a narrative mechanism that can be
called (with lots and lots of definitions and caveats) "typology."

Let's start with the Nephites and the Lamanites. The story
of the Jaredites parallels the story of the Lehites in a dozen
important ways. Both stories begin in biblical settings, before
major catastrophic biblical events involving Babylon (the Tower
of Babel and the Babylonian Captivity). Both center around a
family that is saved from the catastrophe by God's intervention.
Both families build boats and, with the help of God, travel to the
New World, where they split into constantly warring factions.
Ultimately, both societies are destroyed by "secret combinations"
that place the acquisition of wealth above all else.

All of these little bits and pieces of narratives can be called "type scenes," or just "types" that can be removed from one story and reassembled in another—much as the story of Pharaoh's massacre of Hebrew children in Exodus is reassembled to describe Herod's "Massacre of the Innocents" in Matthew. There are reasons—theological, historiographical, and literary—to create and re-use type scenes, which is why they occur so often in the Bible. They help orient readers. They connect different stories together. And they present a God who works in consistent and predictable ways.

And the typology in Ether works in two directions at once. Along with all of the type scenes that connect it to the Lehite narrative, another set of type scenes connects it to the Book of Mormon's origin story. It functions in Mormon's narrative in much the same way that Mormon's narrative functions in the Joseph Smith story. In both stories, the records of a vanished people are hidden by a lone survivor and discovered and translated by prophets through "the gift and power of God." Furthermore, the plates of Ether are hidden with other records in the ground and Mormon is told as a young boy of ten that he will be allowed to retrieve them when he is "about twenty and four years old" (Mor. 1:3). For Joseph, it is fourteen and twenty and two. Easily close enough for a type scene.

And this is why I think that the Book of Ether makes sense where it is. Typologically it tells us two important things: 1) this has all happened before; and 2) this is all going to happen again. Positioned where it is, at the end of Mormon's narrative, just before Moroni says his last words and buries the plates, it can point simultaneously to all that has gone before and all that will come after and assure us that all of sacred history forms, with our own time, a logical continuum governed by a consistent deity and a predictable set of narrative patterns.

# 44

## Moroni's Message in a Bottle: How to (Re) Build a Church

PERHAPS NO CHAPTER IN THE BOOK OF MORMON seems more out of place than the eighth chapter of Moroni. It occurs towards the end of a genocidal campaign against Moroni's people. He is quite likely the last Nephite left on earth. The record has already been completed, and he is now traveling across the hemisphere schlepping about 500 pounds of gold plates and trying to avoid all of the people who want to kill him, which is pretty much everybody. What a strange time to transcribe a letter from his father about infant baptism.

What's going on? The standard Sunday School answer would be that the Lord saw our day and knew that we would struggle with the question of infant baptism, so he inspired Mormon and Moroni to include this epistle. And the standard anti-Mormon answer would be that Joseph Smith was making stuff up to speak to a major religious controversy of his day. Both of these answers, I think, treat the actual text of the Book of Mormon as evidence to support or refute a historical argument.

What I committed to do in this book was to treat the Book of Mormon as a primary text and not as evidence for anything else, and, in this vein, I would like to suggest that there is a textual warrant for this passage that is deeply rooted in one of the major threads of the Book of Mormon. Indeed, it is perhaps the most important narrative thread in the portion that Mormon redacted, namely, the development and preservation of the Nephite Church.

Let's go all the way back to the start of Mormon's redaction. The entire Book of Mosiah is organized around Alma's establishment of a Church, something almost unheard of in the ancient world. The first half of Mosiah maneuvers a group of Nephites into a position—the court of King Noah—where they fall away from the correct belief and are visited by an Old Testament-style prophet. Abinidai preaches and converts Alma, who then converts a group of followers and institutes (perhaps for the first time in the history of the world) the ordinance of baptism, the defining feature of the new Church.

The Church, then, becomes the main character of the Books of Alma and Helaman. For most of this time, it is an official state Church, but, because the Nephites have some kind of religious freedom, people are free to accept or reject it. Alma gives up his political position to win converts to the Church, and the Sons of Mosiah bring a group of Lamanites into the fold. In time, the Church manages to erase the racial divisions between "Nephites" and "Lamanites." In Helaman and the first part of 3 Nephi, the Church falls on hard times and is just about to be wiped out, when the signs of Christ's birth appear and turn the tables on its opponents. Christ comes and sets everything right, leading to 200 years of Utopian bliss.

The foundation of the Nephite Church, then, is the crowning achievement—and the organizing principle—of Mormon's narrative, and it is something that has all but disappeared from the world that he and his son know. In this sense, Mormon and Moroni were in the same position as the Levite priests after the destruction of the Temple in Jerusalem: they were the last initiates into a community of rituals and practices that would disappear from the world unless they wrote everything down.

The Levites produced the Book of Leviticus. Moroni produced the Book of Moroni, which is (thankfully) a much easier book to read, but which serves much the same purpose: they are both instruction manuals on how to build a church written to a future people in the hopes that they will restore what has been lost. The first five chapters of Moroni give the basics: how to confirm someone a member of the Church, how to ordain priests and teachers, how to administer the sacrament. This is the nuts-and-bolts how-to-run-a-church stuff that anybody trying to reassemble what the Nephites built will need to know.

It is in this context that Moroni reproduces his father's epistle on infant baptism. It is a cross-generational team effort between the only two people left in the world who know how to run a Church. Like the Levitical priests, they know (or at least have reason to suspect) that anything they forget to write down will be lost forever. In the same ways that the Levites felt compelled to write down or reproduce every grizzly detail of the animal sacrifices that occurred in the Temple, Moroni felt compelled to say everything he could think to say about the central ordinance of the Church that he knew.

MICHAEL AUSTIN IS THE AUTHOR of seven previous books, including *Rereading Job*, *We Must Not Be Enemies*, and the bestselling textbook, *Reading the World: Ideas that Matter*. Michael is currently the Executive Vice President for Academic Affairs and Provost at Snow College in Ephraim, Utah.

Who hath eyes to see, let them see.

Made in the USA
Las Vegas, NV
08 March 2024

86893677R00152